PROCLAMATION:

Aids for Interpreting the
Lessons of the Church Year

SERIES C

Daniel B. Stevick
and
Ben Johnson

FORTRESS PRESS Philadelphia, Pennsylvania

Library of Congress Catalog Card Number 73-79351

ISBN 0-8006-4054-3

Second printing 1974

4457E74 Printed in U.S.A. 1-4054

General Preface

Proclamation: Aids for Interpreting the Lessons of the Church Year is a series of twenty-five books designed to help clergymen carry out their preaching ministry. It offers exegetical interpretations of the lessons for each Sunday and many of the festivals of the church year, plus homiletical ideas and insights.

The basic thrust of the series is ecumenical. In recent years the Episcopal church, the Roman Catholic church, the United Church of Christ, and the Lutheran and Presbyterian churches have adopted lectionaries that are based on a common three-year system of lessons for the Sundays and festivals of the church year. *Proclamation* grows out of this development, and authors have been chosen from all of these traditions. Some of the contributors are parish pastors; others are teachers, both of biblical interpretation and of homiletics. Ecumenical interchange has been encouraged by putting two persons from different traditions to work on a single volume, one with the primary responsibility for exegesis and the other for homiletical interpretation.

Despite the high percentage of agreement between the traditions, both in the festivals that are celebrated and the lessons that are appointed to be read on a given day, there are still areas of divergence. Frequently the authors of individual volumes have tried to take into account the various textual traditions, but in some cases this has proved to be impossible; in such cases we have felt constrained to limit the material to the Lutheran readings.

The preacher who is looking for "canned sermons" in these books will be disappointed. These books are one step removed from the pulpit: they explain what the lessons are saying and suggest ways of relating this biblical message to the contemporary situation. As such they are springboards for creative thought as well as for faithful proclamation of the word.

This volume of *Proclamation* has been prepared by Daniel B. Stevick, Professor of Homiletics and Worship at the Philadelphia Divinity School,

Philadelphia, Pa., and Benjamin A. Johnson, Professor of New Testament at the Hamma School of Theology of Wittenberg University, Springfield, Ohio. Prof. Stevick was the editor and homiletician and Prof. Johnson was the exegete.

Introduction

Holy Week is often preached through, worshiped through, and lived through in the Christian community as a whole, concentrated sequence. A few words introducing the week as a unit may be in order.

Each Holy Week invites the preacher and the congregation (and, for that matter, the authors of this booklet) to be coexplorers into the death of Jesus. That death is told and proclaimed among those who are convinced that it is significant; it is gospel. The institutional supports of liturgy, hymn, official roles, art, and dogma all insist that the death of Jesus is meaningful. But neither our own need to find it meaningful nor the external pressures of Christian culture, which adds its testimony that Jesus' death makes sense, should let us take shortcuts in this exploration. Before the death of Jesus became part of a revelation or a gospel, it was an event—a stark, brutal death. Before the faith of the cross had called a community into being, the cross was the experience—in desolating solitude—of one man. The first context in which the death was assimilated by others was the awareness of its horror and disillusion. We know the one who died; and such a death of such a person strikes us first as evidence of tragic waste, of senselessness, of cosmic injustice. If it says anything about Jesus, it is only that the best die as meanly as the worst. If it has any effect for persons in general, it is to diminish the sense of their worth. Only after we have seen this event as evidence of meaninglessness can we appreciate the revolution that the resurrection faith and the gospel of Christ crucified represent.

This movement in Holy Week, into death and towards resurrection, to faith by way of despair, is not accessible to biblical scholarship, in the sense of a study of primary records in their historical setting. It cannot be a professional preaching matter first—can a busy pastor find a series of sermons for the week? It cannot ask the secondhand question, What did the death of Jesus mean to Paul, Irenaeus, Augustine, Thomas, Luther, Calvin, Cranmer, Wesley, or their successors of our own day? We cannot ask what it has meant to unreflective people of faith, in our own and other ages. In Holy Week, we must ask freshly what Jesus' death means this year to me, in the depths of my existence. The tools of such inquiry are honesty, openness to new possibility, willingness to set aside cherished ideas if they are inadequate, ability to look at familiar events with fresh eyes, courage to judge ourselves and be judged.

Such an exploration gives us back what we have set aside in order to make it. We as students are in touch with the witness literature of the Bible because we have faced the question it faces. We as preachers have something to say. We as believers are set within a great community of faith and interpretation.

The authors of this booklet cannot claim to have gone very far in such an exploration—still less that these comments will provide more than hints for others. We only observe that this work has confronted us again with the crucial events of the faith and the ultimate issues of life and death. This biblical material has its own power and authority. The one on whom it centers still declares himself to those who rehearse his story.

We have not sought to develop any part of the material fully. Rather, the sections that follow are meant to leave a reader (especially a preacher) with a great deal of work of his own to do. But if we can start a few lines of productive thought for others, our aim will have been accomplished.

Unfortunately for an ecumenical series, the readings in the various churches' lectionaries diverge more during Holy Week than during other parts of the church year. Some of the passages in the Lutheran lectionary are used by some of the other churches, but more are not. This volume of *Proclamation* may present difficulties for non-Lutheran users. The authors wish it had been possible to do more to bring this discrepant material together for the church's worship and preaching during this week of all weeks.

Daniel B. Stevick

Table of Contents

The Sunday of the Passion, Palm Sunday

Lutheran	*Roman Catholic*	*Episcopal*	*Presbyterian and UCC*
Deut. 32:36–39	Isa. 50:4–7	Zech. 9:9–12	Isa. 59:14–20
Phil. 2:5–11	Phil. 2:6–11	Phil. 2:5–11	1 Tim. 1:12–17
Luke 22:1–23:56	Luke 22:14–23:55	Luke 22:39–23:49	Luke 19:28–40

EXEGESIS

First Lesson: Deut. 32:36–39. This section is taken from the song of Moses which stands near the end of the book of Deuteronomy. If Deuteronomy is a compendium of Mosaic theology presented in sermonic form, then this psalm stands in relation to it as a well-chosen hymn stands in relation to a sermon. It asserts Israel's responsibility for its present difficulties, but promises eventual vindication at God's hands.

The context is one of theoretical polytheism and functional monotheism. Yahweh chides his people for placing confidence in the gods resident in the land. He seems to credit such gods with enough reality to receive the meat and drink of offerings (v. 38). But he is equally confident that they are impotent to help the people. His challenge to them in the last part of v. 38 can be imagined to have been followed by a heavy silence.

That silence is the transition to the climax of the passage. "See now that I, even I, am he, and there is no god beside me." The absence of power among the other gods brings from Yahweh the assertion of their nonreality. Only Yahweh is worthy of consideration because it is he who is the source of all of life's forces. And in the parallelism of v. 39*b* he lays claim to be the active agent in bringing about death and life, injury and health. And in the fashion of a predator he hurls the final challenge of the verse, "there is none that can deliver out of my hand."

Yahweh's relation to the other gods and nations and to a disobedient Israel has something of the character of a cat playing with a mouse. While it may appear that Israel is going her own way, that the weaker gods of the nation have the upper hand, it is only because Yahweh is allowing it to happen. Ultimate power resides in his paws and all the world is no farther away than one bound.

In such an actice view of the power of God and the weakness of his rivals for power, there is a strong pressure to read all events as occurring in accordance with his will, to say that even what appears senseless makes sense, at least to Yahweh. To what extent such a doctrine of God does credit to him is another question.

Second Lesson: Phil. 2:5–11. This text represents one of the few occasions when Paul speaks for some few sentences about the life of Jesus. It has been a source of some confusion among interpreters that Paul would in what is essentially a hortatory section of his letter launch into a theological exposition. This confusion has been resolved to some extent by the discovery by Johannes Weiss at the turn of the century that Phil. 2:6–11*a* is a primitive Christian hymn, a piece of preformed Christian devotion to which Paul appealed.

The hymn itself is generally understood to celebrate Christ's voluntary subordination to God, a subordination in which he took human form and became obedient unto death. As a reward for this act of subordination and obedience God highly exalted him and makes all creation sing his praise.

The origins of such a mythological interpretation of Jesus have been sought by interpreters in Iran, Greek philosophy, mystery religions, the emperor cult, Hellenistic Judaism, and various other systems of thought or myth. (For a detailed study of modern interpretation of this passage see R. P. Martin's *Carmen Christi: Philippians Two:5–11* [New York: Cambridge University Press, 1967].) The values held up in the passage fit well with the Judaism from which Christianity sprang. See for instance the following parallelism.

ADAM	*CHRIST*
Made in the divine image	Being the image of God
thought it a prize to be grasped at	thought it not a prize to be grasped at
to be as God;	to be as God;
and aspired to a reputation	and made himself of no reputation
and spurned being God's servant	and took upon Him the form of a servant
seeking to be in the likeness of God;	and was made in the likeness of men;

and being found in fashion as a man (of dust, now doomed), he exalted himself, and became disobedient unto death. He was condemned and disgraced.	and being found in fashion as a man (Rom. viii. 3) He humbled Himself, and became obedient unto death. God highly exalted Him and gave Him the name and rank of Lord.[1]

What is most striking here is the comparison which Paul implies. Our interest is primarily his use of the material and not its origin. What the preexistent Christ and the Philippians have in common is a lofty position and a sovereign will. There is no sense in which Paul would wish to achieve his goal, namely, that the Philippians show mutual concern, by belittling them or giving them commands. They are free and worthy.

In that, they are like Christ. But then Paul appeals to what Christ did with his lofty position and sovereign will. He emptied himself and became obedient—not because it was his natural or rightful condition, but because it was what he wished. And it paid off in even greater glory. So ought the Philippians to conduct themselves.

Gospel: Luke 22:1–23:56. The story of Luke 22:1–23 is a story of the plot against Jesus. Within it is set the story of Jesus' arrangements for and celebration of the Passover (vv. 7–19), which will be treated in detail in the section on Maundy Thursday. Here the focus is on plots and intrigues, on stealth and strange bedfellows.

The largest social grouping represented by Luke in this story is "the people" (v. 2; cf. 21:38). The struggle for the hearts and minds of the people was being won by Jesus. Hence he represented to existing leadership groups a threat to their power and position.

Luke tells in v. 1 of the coming together of two of these groups, the chief priests of the Sadducean party (cf. Acts 5:17) and the scribes (very likely designating the educated among the popular lay reform party, the Pharisees), around their opposition to Jesus. In like manner he represents Pilate and Herod coming together around a common attitude toward Jesus (23:6–12).

In counterpoint to the coming together of competing leadership groups in their opposition to Jesus, we read in v. 3 that "Satan entered into

1. R. P. Martin, *Carmen Christi: Philippians Two:5–11* (New York: Cambridge University Press, 1967), pp. 163–64.

Judas Iscariot, who was one of the twelve." The handing over of Jesus, the diminishing of his power and the assertion of those aligned against him, is made possible by a break in the solidarity of his community.

The reasons for the betrayal of Jesus by Judas have been a subject for speculation from the earliest days of the church. The account in Mark 14:10–11 simply declares that Judas volunteered to betray Jesus, and that in gratitude the leaders offered money. Matt. 26:14–16 makes it a straight business transaction, where Judas asks, "What will you give me if I betray him?" In John 12:4–8 a history of avarice and theft is attributed to Judas. A second stream in the understanding of Judas is represented in John 13:2, 27 and Luke 22:3, the verse before us. The prince of demons is the effective cause behind Judas's betrayal.

The first reason seems trifling for one whose life had been touched by Jesus and the second unsatisfying to anyone who asks, Why Judas and not one of the other disciples? Because of this, the motives of Judas have remained one of the most fascinating areas for Christian speculation through the ages, right down to *Jesus Christ Superstar.*

Seen from the perspective of the plot against Jesus, the preparation for the celebration of the Passover and the celebration itself provide a platform for the storyteller's communication to the hearer that the plot against Jesus did not contravene the intention of Jesus or the purposes of God.

Vv. 7 ff. also represent a return to a focus on Jesus. While the words "the day on which the Passover lamb had to be slaughtered" are probably an unweighted explanation for Gentile readers, they cannot fail to suggest potentially rich lines of interpretation of Jesus as the paschal lamb.

The mysterious advance arrangements for a Passover celebration within the confines of the Holy City remain mysterious. Had Jesus made advance arrangements? Was this an exercise of his amazing powers of prescience? Is the hand of God at work here? Whatever the reason, Jesus and his disciples would have their place.

That place is Jesus' setting for his interpretation of what is unfolding. This interpretation involves three elements: (1) Jesus wants his last meal with the disciples to be one of solemn ceremony, appropriate to the investment he has had in their life together; (2) he will never again eat the Passover until it is fulfilled in the kingdom of God (v. 16); and (3) there is a connection between his death and their fellowship (vv. 17–19).

This particular segment of the story is enormously complex in its history and textual transmission. Joachim Jeremias's *The Eucharistic Words of Jesus* (Naperville, Ill.: Alec R. Allenson, 1966) offers an excellent resource for further reading concerning this matter. At least four meals are involved: (1) Jesus' ordinary table-fellowship with his disciples (but how could that have been ordinary when in the company of Jesus?); (2) the Passover celebration, which calls to mind God's deliverance of his people from Egypt; (3) the messianic banquet of the future, which is alluded to when Jesus speaks of eating the meal again in the kingdom of God; and (4) the eucharistic meal of the early church, which is reflected particularly in vv. 17–19*a* (and 19*b*–20, whether these verses are from Luke's hand or that of later editors). In any event, the disciples are important to Jesus. There is promise of life beyond death and destruction. The attempts of the opposition to destroy the meaning of Jesus will fail.

In the last section (vv. 21–23) the contrapuntal movement of this segment is brought together in one sentence spoken by Jesus, "For the Son of man is going his appointed way; but alas for that man by whom he is betrayed!" Taking the second half first, we can see it as a naked assertion of human responsibility and accountability for acts of evil. Judas is responsible for the death of Jesus and will pay for that betrayal with his own life (see Acts 1:13). Both the story of Judas hanging himself (Matt. 27:3–10) and the Acts story of his bursting open are stories of self-destruction, not divine retribution.

In spite of the efforts of the leaders in collusion with Judas, they were unable to frustrate the will of God and the intention of Jesus. "The Son of man is going his appointed way" is an affirmation that the death of Jesus does make sense in relation to a cosmic drama in which Luke sees both Satan and God in the wings. A more precise idea of the sense it makes may unfold as the week progresses.

HOMILETICAL INTERPRETATION

The OT reading speaks of God as judge. It is part of an extended lawsuit section (32:1–43) in which heaven and earth as jury (v. 1) hear an account of God's faithfulness to his people and of Israel's disobedience. God speaks in the role of witness against his people for most of the chapter. But in these verses, he fills the role of judge. Not only has the role changed, but so has the tone. God as judge is not impartial—above the affairs of history, settling accounts disinterestedly at the end. Rather, God is depicted in biblical terms as participant, as deeply involved. He chooses, he loves, he cares. He is the judge who vindicates his people. He is partisan; he takes their side; he is *for* them. His judgment is his loving-kindness.

What is the appeal on the basis of which God can vindicate? He has himself cited the long record of his people's waywardness. (See parallels, especially chap. 1 of Isaiah, in which lawsuit imagery is used to arraign the people of God.) Yet he finds in their behalf when he sees that his people are powerless. Their own strength is gone. The false gods in which they trusted—as Yahweh notes tauntingly—are discredited. When all else has failed and his people are weak, vulnerable, and chastened, the bond with the true and living God stands. When the nation was strong and successful, it forsook God; but in its weakness, with its false gods fallen, it can turn only to the true Rock, who stands forth alone. (Note the vivid self-assertion in v. 39: "I, even I, am he, and there is no god beside me.") He is the self-existent, the one, the living God who confronts persons as an "I." (Compare: "I am the Lord your God who brought you out of the land of Egypt"; "I will be what I will be.") He is the one who asserts his power and competence in the midst of our despair and confusion.

The OT lesson may well set some of the themes of Holy Week: God as vindicator; God vindicating just at the point at which man on his own is most confounded, when the gods of his own choosing have failed him; God as one who testifies against a people who have misplaced their reliance, but who reveals himself in compassion and power in behalf of those to whom he has bound himself when they know themselves to be powerless.

The dramatic sweep and poetic form of the passage from Philippians suggest that it is indeed a christological hymn. It has two general movements, downward and upward. In a few short lines it tells the story of Christ, who, existing in the form of God, emptied himself and took on himself the role of man; as man he accepted the mission of a servant, obedient unto death. Then in another set of short lines, God is spoken of as exalting Christ and giving him a name which ultimately all the universe will acknowledge.

Although the hymn speaks in terms of Christ alone (the humiliation

ory of the fall
at he did has
r humanity, an

course, at the
ative connota-
mmitment are
ne who lived,
an account of
is it proof of
ld not be con-
y. The church
ves—Lord over
ontinuous with
lted one. "God
you crucified."
claration could
n reaches back-
contradiction,
action of God.
s, so to speak,
church which
cal speculation
r, the creative,
ing movement
e obstinacy of
oses. The story
es, places, con-
ther story. Its
urpose of God,

iorities of life.
d one—is cited
owed little re-
tructive of the
vas evidence of
rce the simple
n about Christ

as model of the servant-pa
in Christ Jesus." What is
munity is desired can be
role of a member of the
with respect to oneself an
chastened self-regard, a s
investment of oneself in t
and to sacrifice.

The point of this hymn
asks of us nothing that
makes no demands of us
enabling. In a sense, Chri
incarnation. The central,
interpersonal attitudes. Of
Christ's role was unique a
one—the one who though
Christ's to share and ours
gift, a fellowship, a unity,
Let what he thought be th

The Gospel passage be
which is called the Passov
7–13, 14 f.). Both the Las
acted against the backgrou
(vv. 1, 6) are the pilgrims
among the disciples was n
of retirement in the crow
would not cause a tumult
ments, a room in which t
yond such circumstances
conflict with his enemies
awareness that this is all
over.

But what was and is th
of Judaism. The observan
that it goes back to a Can
most fundamental new dep
it a memorial of a historic
mental context of life, in

and the exaltation are his), the implied inversion of the story of the fall suggests much more. Christ is not an individual hero. What he did has importance for the race; he is a new Adam, a fresh start for humanity, an undoing of the primal sin, a declaration of true lordship.

This "mythological" interpretation of Christ began, of course, at the center and worked in both directions from there. (No negative connotation attaches to the term "myth." Ultimate meaning and commitment are expressible in no other way.) Jesus was first known as one who lived, taught the kingdom, and was crucified. This in itself is an account of tragic waste, woven into the pattern of human affairs (or is it proof of their moral patternlessness?). But that bit of history could not be confined to history. The hymn leaps forward beyond history. The church knew and knows the one who died to be the one who lives—Lord over all, and pledge of God's ultimate triumph. The cross was continuous with the self-vindication of God; the crucified one was the exalted one. "God has made him both Lord and Christ, this Jesus whom you crucified." But what so clearly belonged to the center of God's self-declaration could not but have roots in an eternal purpose to save. The hymn reaches backward beyond history. The death on a cross—the curse, the contradiction, the scandal—becomes a revelation of the character and action of God. Mythical terms seek to capture something which belongs, so to speak, both to the history of man and to the history of God. The church which composed this hymn was not interested in the theological speculation which such language could not help but evoke. Rather, the creative, image-making community was declaring a gospel, a sweeping movement which began and ended in God and which engaged the obstinacy of human history in working out his long-laid saving purposes. The story of Jesus and his cross belongs to our world of events, times, places, conflicts, tears, outrage. But it is also the midpoint of another story. Its fullest context is in the eternal and ultimately victorious purpose of God, who is mighty to save.

Deeply felt myths express meaning and govern the priorities of life. This myth of Christ—the self-humbling and God-exalted one—is cited here with an ethical intent. Some Christians at Philippi showed little regard for one another. Their self-centeredness proved destructive of the life of the new community. The wish to dominate others was evidence of the sinful, self-seeking Adam role. Paul sought to enforce the simple lesson of humility and considerateness by this mighty hymn about Christ as model of the servant-pattern. "Let this mind be in you which was also in Christ Jesus." What is wanted at Philippi and wherever sound community is desired can be described in terms of traits of character. The role of a member of the fellowship in Christ requires a certain "mind" with respect to oneself and the purposes of existence—a responsible and chastened self-regard, a spontaneous identification with others, a joyful investment of oneself in their well-being, a willingness to give, to serve, and to sacrifice.

The point of this hymn about Christ is, in Paul's context, that Christ asks of us nothing that he has not pioneered and demonstrated. He makes no demands of us for which his own redemptive work is not an enabling. In a sense, Christians are, in this passage, asked to imitate the incarnation. The central, saving action of Christ is made the model for interpersonal attitudes. Of course, in one sense such a thing is absurd; Christ's role was unique and inimitable. But the "mind" of the incarnate one—the one who though he was rich became poor for our sake—is Christ's to share and ours to receive. It is more than a model. It is a gift, a fellowship, a unity, a participation. "Let Christ's mind be in you." Let what he thought be thought by you—indeed, let him think it in you.

The Gospel passage begins with the words, "Now the feast drew near which is called the Passover." Luke emphasizes the Passover setting (vv. 7–13, 14 f.). Both the Last Supper and the entire passion story are enacted against the background of Jerusalem at Passover. "The multitude" (vv. 1, 6) are the pilgrims in the city for the religious festival. A traitor among the disciples was needed by Jesus' enemies to point out his place of retirement in the crowded city and to do it at a time when arrest would not cause a tumult. Jesus sought, apparently by secret arrangements, a room in which to eat the Passover with his followers. But beyond such circumstances as these, the whole spiritual drama of Jesus' conflict with his enemies and his ultimate death is heightened by the awareness that this is all taking place at no ordinary time, but at Passover.

But what was and is the Passover? It is the greatest religious festival of Judaism. The observance itself is very old, and there are indications that it goes back to a Canaanite agricultural festival. But, in one of the most fundamental new departures in religious history, the Hebrews made it a memorial of a historic event, the deliverance from Egypt. The fundamental context of life, in the biblical view, is not man-in-nature, but man-in-history. God declares himself not in natural cycles but in mighty deeds of choosing, calling, saving, judging. At a moment, God had acted to emancipate his people, to bring them into covenant with himself, to lead them by his hand as pilgrims through the wilderness, and to bring them to their land. The Passover spoke for all of this: "And when in time to come your son asks you, 'What does this mean?' you shall say to him, 'By strength of hand the Lord brought us out of Egypt, from the house of bondage.' "

For the Hebrew, as year by year he remembered the saving event, it was made present. Time was obliterated; we were in our fathers, and they were in us. The Passover was a recalling and renewing of the covenant. The event, its power and its meaning, were not distant and dim; they were once again present realities. The Mishnah, in famous words, comments: "In every generation a man must so regard himself as if he came forth himself out of Egypt."

The exegetical comments have indicated that, seen at close range, this week in Jesus' life is a story of intrigue and secrecy, of developments which Jesus did not seek and from which he shrank. The joy of Jesus' enemies that they had found a traitor among the disciples and the mention of a payment of money (v. 5) give evidence of a sordid business. The prearranged signals and passwords (vv. 7–13) indicate the secret measures Jesus was required to take to secure an undisturbed place for his last meal with his disciples. This close-range view is valuable. If, in the events of Holy Week, man's redemption was won, those events were part of the ordinary texture of history: official rejection of an unofficial, provocative leader; isolation, foreboding; the search for privacy amid tension and swirling events; conflict and misunderstanding; close fellowship, plotting; loyalty and treachery.

But the story of Holy Week is told in the gospels (and retold and relived in the church) by those who see it from a long-range perspective. It is the story of the final conflict and death of one who is known as living Lord. That ugly, tragic knot of human history that led to the cross has been transformed into a gospel of triumph and salvation.

In looking at Holy Week from this long-range view of faith, few factors have provided more categories for its interpretation than the simple fact that it fell on Passover. The final conflict, suffering, and death of Christ coincided with the great Jewish festival of emancipation from Egypt.

As seen by the eyes of faith, this coincidence is of the utmost significance for stating what has been made possible for mankind through Christ. He is interpreted in terms of the exodus and the Passover. Jesus has broken the yoke of the profoundest and most universal slavery—bondage to sin. The true sacrifice has been made. History's real Passover has been celebrated. A new covenant people has been brought into a relation with God—made kings and priests. A new age has dawned. A new festival meal has been provided. A pilgrim people follows the will of God and trusts in his provision. A promised land is pledged.

In the early church, these figures and themes were gathered up and repeated in connection with the great yearly paschal observance. God had brought his people from bondage to freedom, from darkness into light, from this world of death to resurrection in the world to come.

The time reference with which Luke 22 opens can sound like a bit of chronology intended to set the last days of Jesus against an important public event. The reference to the Passover does that, but it does much more. It gives a connection from which much of the evangelical and theological interpretation of the meaning of Jesus Christ and his cross has been derived. The sum of redemption is "Christ our Passover has been sacrificed." "Behold the Lamb of God."

In our time, people hunger for freedom, for purpose, for true community, for hope. These rightful parts of the human inheritance are secured in Christ; in him we have them and celebrate them as a present reality; we are committed to bringing them into the lives of our fellowmen. The message of the Passover—the OT festival fulfilled and reinterpreted in Christ—is good news. It speaks of the transformation of the human situation.

The part of the Gospel for Passion Sunday which refers specifically to the Last Supper (vv. 7–20) is repeated as the liturgical Gospel for Maundy Thursday. Exegetical and homiletical comments on the Lucan account of the meal will be found in the pages of this booklet devoted to that day's readings.

The Gospel reading for today devotes some attention to Judas (vv. 3–5, 21–23; more material on Judas occurs in the Gospel for Wednesday in Holy Week.) Judas and his motives have been a subject for much speculation. But he remains a mystery to us—as possibly he was to the evangelists. Despite some useful conjectures, there is no satisfactory explanation of Judas. He confronts us with the mystery of evil—in history and in ourselves—and he shares in its inexplicable character. Luke stresses the tragic fact that treachery came from Jesus' inner circle: "Judas called Iscariot, who was of the number of the twelve"; "the hand of him who betrays me is with me on the table." Luke attributes Judas' act to Satan (v. 3). Two kingdoms had been at war throughout Jesus' ministry; here Satan's kingdom found an accomplice in the circle closest to Jesus. Jesus senses the alienation of Judas and speaks of his purposes without accusing him or mentioning him by name. It is striking that none of the other disciples suspected Judas. Yet apparently they were all willing to suspect themselves.

Monday in Holy Week

Lutheran	*Roman Catholic*	*Episcopal*	*Presbyterian and UCC*
Isa. 42:1–9	Isa. 42:1–7	Isa. 42:1–7	Isa. 50:4–10
Heb. 9:11–15		Heb. 11:39–12:3	Heb. 9:11–15
John 12:1–11	John 12:1–11	John 12:1–11 (Mark 14:3–9)	Luke 19:41–48

EXEGESIS

First Lesson: Isa. 42:1–9. The OT lessons for four of the six days in this series are the four servant songs embedded in Second Isaiah. Some general comments will be made here, applicable to all four songs (42:1–9; 49:1–6; 50:4–9; and 52:13–53:12).

One of the best-established critical results of modern biblical scholarship has been the recognition of a second writer's work in the book of Isaiah. This second writer, the so-called Second Isaiah or Deutero-Isaiah, flourished during the latter part of the Babylonian captivity (the second half of the sixth century B.C.) and was the prophet of restoration and return. He is almost universally credited with chaps. 40–55. Some commentators assign to him chaps. 35 (36) and 56–66 as well. Others opt for a Third Isaiah or at least separate authorship for 56–66, which is judged to reflect the period after the return. However, the four sections with which we are concerned all fall within that portion attributed to Second Isaiah.

Within Second Isaiah four units can be isolated which treat of Ebed Yahweh, the servant of the Lord. They are self-contained, although interspersed throughout chaps. 40–45. They are one of the most hotly contested portions of the OT. The earlier debate was between Christian interpreters who understood these songs as a clear reference to Jesus and Jewish interpreters who perceived the servant as a figure which referred to all Israel. More recently lines have been less obviously confessionally drawn with the decline of a straight christological interpretation of the OT. Yet the representative understanding has continued strong while those who understand the servant as an individual have sought the individual with which to identify him. Moses, Jeremiah, Jehoiachim, Zerubbabel, a teacher of the Torah, and an unknown contemporary martyr are among the nominations, as well as the most obvious, Deutero-Isaiah himself.

An apparent solution to this critical impasse in the identification of the servant is given a context in H. Wheeler Robinson's *Corporate Personality in Ancient Israel* (originally published in 1935; reprinted in the Fortress Press Facet Books series in 1964). Robinson explains that in Hebrew thought, communities could be spoken of as having personal qualities and could be seen through representative individuals. He calls this feature of OT thought "corporate personality." "In the light of this conception the Servant can be both the prophet himself as representative of the nation, and the nation whose proper mission is actually being fulfilled only by the prophet and that group of followers who may share his views."[1] At the very least the prophet's sense of identity and mission is profoundly shaped by his corporate sense of himself and Israel.

The first song (42:1–9) paints a picture of the servant which is sustained throughout the songs. He is not like Cyrus, the benevolent warrior that God is using to accomplish his purposes. Like Cyrus he *is* an agent of justice. But he is soft-spoken (v. 2) and gentle (v. 3). Yet his mission is no less grandiose than that of Cyrus. He will "plant justice on earth" (v. 4). He has been chosen by the Lord to be "a light to all peoples, a beacon for the nations" (v. 6, NEB). His activity will also have specific social significance: the opening of the eyes of the blind and the release of captives.

1. H. Wheeler Robinson, *Corporate Personality in Ancient Israel*, Facet Books, Biblical Series, no. 11 (Philadelphia: Fortress Press, 1964), p. 15.

Yahweh is represented as concerned that he himself receive proper credit for the things about to happen. He points to the success of previously announced prophecies to validate those now announced. The imagery is of springtime ("before they break from the bud").

Second Lesson: Heb. 9:11–15. The theology of the book of Hebrews is, from one perspective, one of the most clear and consistently worked out of the entire Bible. The writing is high, noble, and has a capacity to carry the reader along with it. The author is a reflective person, well studied in the OT but with an apparent distance from the Jewish community. (He does not anguish, like Paul in Rom. 9–11, over what his theology means for the Jewish nation.)

It is more difficult to sort out what precisely the author's questions were and how he understood the OT to be answering them. His claim seems to be that the bloody death of Jesus was a final, fully efficacious sacrifice for sin for those who are obedient to him (5:8–9). As a fully efficacious sacrifice it also removes any sense of sin, or brings the worshipers to perfection (10:1–3). But such a host of blessings it can only deliver once. If people fall away after "they have had a taste of the heavenly gift and a share in the Holy Spirit" (6:4), it is impossible for them to come again to repentance. Because of this rigorist position the book was unpopular in some circles. The Shepherd of Hermas, a second-century document reputed to have been written in Rome, participated in the same general kind of ingroup/outgroup thinking but allowed for a second repentance. The eventual development of the penitential system gave more flexibility to this general mind-set.

The particular text before us here can be approached in two ways. One can ask about what the author means when he says that "Jesus' blood will cleanse our conscience from the deadness of our former ways and fit us for the service of the living God" (9:14). The blood (death) of Jesus establishes an inward righteousness among his followers. This may mean that the death itself freed God to dispense the Holy Spirit, who in turn would provide the sinless state for those who are brought into the new covenant. Still that seems a strange mixing of mechanical (sacrificial system) and ethical (conscience) metaphors. To make sense of Jesus' death today we need to interpret it not through the ancient cult of animal sacrifice or even some hypothetical needs of God to satisfy his own righteousness. Rather the death of Jesus needs to be interpreted in terms of his own life and the forces that moved to oppose him. Those forces were said to have survived him, even as his disciples provided testimony that he survived death. An unraveling of those forces and factors will give us a clue to the staying power of Jesus. And it will enable us to make judgments on the ethical/communal level prior to considering the question in terms of extrapolations about the plan and purpose of God.

Gospel: John 12:1–11. The story of the anointing of Jesus is found in all four gospels (Mark 14:3–9; Matt. 26:6–13; Luke 7:36–50). It is a story of absorbing interest both in its history and its impact.

First, a few comments on its history. (Here I am indebted to David Daube's article on the story in the *Anglican Theological Review* 32 [1950]: 186–99.) The earliest version of this story is probably Luke 7:37–38. A woman on a certain occasion expressed her love for Jesus (and perhaps her own feelings of unworthiness) by spending her money on some precious ointment and using it to cleanse and soften Jesus' feet.

In all of the gospels the story has been developed controversially. In Luke, Jesus is criticized for allowing a sinner to touch him (7:39). In Mark, Matthew, and John the act itself is attacked as a waste of something valuable which could better have been distributed among the poor. Note that the critics are different in each gospel: in Luke, a Pharisee; in Mark, an indefinite "some of them"; in Matthew, the disciples; and in John, Judas. This is rich material in which to see the interconnectedness of material in the four gospels.

Within the Gospel of John itself, the story has been well integrated. Only a bit before (11:1 ff.) we read of how Jesus reacts to news of the illness of his friend Lazarus. We are all aware of the outcome of that story, the joy it brought to the two sisters, Martha and Mary. On the darker side, however, such a spectacular miracle led many more to believe in Jesus and heightened the resolve of Jewish leadership to do away with him. In any event, when Jesus returns to Bethany to be entertained in the home of Lazarus it does not seem at all surprising that Mary would outdo herself in trying to show her gratitude to Jesus for bringing her brother back from the dead. A happy scene. The turmoil of that now almost unbelievable death and burial is now past.

But two menaces were near at hand. The one could not wait until the supper ended, but came like the atmosphere of an ugly conference luncheon descending upon that carefree and celebrative meal. Judas could not bear to see the costly ointment wasted on Jesus. Yes Judas was there. He could not bear to be indolently happy for a few short hours. (Have you tried that test? "Is it I, Lord?") But what of his complaint? Granted that his timing could not have been worse, what does one say to his charge that this ointment ought to have been sold and distributed to the poor? John solves the problem fairly easily, at least on the surface, by impugning Judas's motives. He only wanted to get that money into the common purse where he could steal some of it.

We need, however, only to look at Mark and Matthew to know that the same question was raised by people who had no such ulterior motives. How could one possibly justify such extravagance? Jesus' answer is represented by v. 8: "The poor you always have with you. But you don't always have me." It is Jesus' affirmation of himself and with that self, all those selves to follow. It says nothing against the poor nor against the disciples' commitment to the poor. But it stakes out a place at the center of Christianity for a celebrative devotion to one another which does not count the cost. And no Judas, with good intentions or bad, can carve that out and throw it away.

The second menace to the joy of the occasion waited just outside. The Gospel of John develops two themes in parallel lines: the growing success of Jesus among the people and the growing opposition to him among the leadership (5:16; 7:1, 13, 49; 10:39; 11:53). People often wonder what happened to Lazarus. While John does not tell us in precise terms, the ominous resolve of the leadership in v. 10 to do away with Lazarus as well as Jesus shows us what John thought of his future chances.

HOMILETICAL INTERPRETATION

The OT reading introduces the mysterious yet powerfully depicted figure, the servant of God. Today's reading specifically sets forth the servant's call and the purposes of his redemptive ministry. The writer represents God as the speaker, as though he were presenting his servant and commending him.

The servant is chosen by God, upheld by his spirit, and is one in whom God delights. The public work of the servant, in other words, derives from an unshared personal depth where one is known, affirmed, empowered, and commissioned by God alone. The fundamental secret of the servant's character is accounted for by the depth of his relation to God.

The servant acts in the power of God, but he acts gently. His manner is unobtrusive, not self-advertising, denunciatory, or tyrannical. He appreciates and cherishes life where he finds it. It may be only as strong as a bent blade of grass or as a lamp which is almost extinguished, but he respects it. The servant takes damaged human material and transforms it.

The purpose of the Creator is the enlightenment and liberation (the two figures are interwoven) of all persons. He seeks people in terms of their need, and he offers his life, his breath, his power to make new. God's servant is set as a sign of God's universal care and love—"a light to the nations." If God calls a person, it is for the sake of the called community and ultimately for the sake of all people. God's election and calling cannot be confined. They are his way of relating persons to his universal, saving purposes. The particular person, in the depth of his individuality, is summoned by God. That calling often leads to pain, misunderstanding, inner correction and teaching. But the individual is never an end in himself; the one is for the sake of the many. God seeks ultimately the renewal, the reclamation of all.

This passage brings together themes which are interrelated in the biblical revelation at its highest, but which are often separated: the electing purpose of God, a gentleness of method, freedom and justice for all people, and the demonstration of the glory of God. History is full of parties which have used the sense of divine calling as an excuse for oppression and a claim to exclusiveness and privilege. Persons who think of themselves as striving for the glory of God have not always sought that end by gentle means. The quest for justice and the love for quiet persuasion have often been mutually incompatible. But "what God hath joined together . . ." In this passage, the purpose and glory of God is man set free and practicing justice. And that aim is brought about by the quiet methods which let human beings reach free human ends by freely chosen human means.

To turn to the Second Lesson, the letter to the Hebrews makes one point repeatedly: the world of the really real had been expressed by shadows in the temple cultus of the OT. But in the events of Christ's life, death, and entry—as Lord and brother—on his continuing heavenly work, the really real had directly, decisively, and finally acted in behalf of man. Since the shadow-images of the temple were God-given, effective though limited, and expressive of the way of redemption, they are a source for understanding the character of the absolute revelation in

Christ—the reality of which the OT system was an inferior and partial representation.

In today's passage, the author argues that the entry of Christ upon his heavenly work was the inauguration of a true high-priesthood, in a real tabernacle (heaven), presenting there a perfect sacrifice (his own blood), and winning a final redemption. If the old ritual really cleansed, the blood of Christ does so "much more." The animal sacrifices provided under the law cleansed the "flesh"; Christ's blood cleanses the conscience.

This early Christian theology indicates the finality and glory of the work of Christ for the faith of the early church. Yet the idiom poses undeniable difficulties for reading and preaching today. The following line of thought may be helpful:

In this passage, the blood of Christ is prominent (vv. 12, 14). The background of this imagery is the ritual use of blood to cleanse from defilement and restore relation with God. This idea of the application of the blood of a sacrifice for the removal of sin can sound remote in the twentieth century and seem to reach only a low level of spiritual insight. But when the author of Hebrews speaks of Christ as a high priest who offered his own blood, he means something special—certainly something nonmagical. Throughout this writing, the term "blood" refers to Christ's entire life of obedience to God and leadership of his brothers. In 10:4–10, the author argues that the sacrifice of an animal cannot remove the sins of a person. Therefore Christ was not one who made the sacrifices in which God could take no pleasure. Rather, Christ was dedicated to doing the will of God. The author explains the contrast by an OT citation: "Sacrifices and offering thou hast not desired, but a body hast thou prepared for me; in burnt offerings and sin offerings thou hast taken no pleasure. Then I said, 'Lo, I have come to do thy will, O God.' " Jesus' sacrifice, or, on this statement of the matter, his "blood," was his life spent in the will of God. Elsewhere the author emphasizes that doing the will of God was costly to Jesus; it involved struggle; when it came to the passion events, Jesus shrank from what lay before him (see, for example, 5:7, 8). Yet through it all he "learned obedience" and was faithful. Thus the form of the priestly model of making sacrifice and purifying by blood is filled in Hebrews with the content of the prophetic model of one called in the midst of historic existence to learn and follow the will of God through difficulty and uncertainty. The source of the world's redemption, in Hebrews, is a life offered to God, lived in the midst of sin, and faithful unto death. The final sacrifice is the life of perfect obedience. Jesus' "sacrifice" (thus defined) united man with God and makes possible the service of the living God (v. 14). The term "service" is a liturgical word. It can be translated "worship" somewhat as in English we speak of going to a church "service." Jesus' own life of faithful obedience, which was his "sacrifice," made a difference for others. It can be duplicated by those who now will follow where he led —worshiping in and through serving.

The passage from John brings these matters of servanthood and sacrifice into close connection with the story of Jesus. The incident of John 12:1–11 comes in the midst of the thickening plot of Holy Week. The reference to the Passover here (v. 1) is probably symbolically loaded. Lazarus is mentioned (vv. 1, 2, 9 f.); the raising of Lazarus is crucial in the drama of the Fourth Gospel; by this account, both Jesus and Lazarus are under sentence of death (11:55–57; 12:10, 11). The forward references to Judas's betrayal (v. 4) and Jesus' burial (v. 7) set this incident as a prelude to the events that are to follow. In this gospel, the anointing at Bethany is probably thought of as an act of devotion to the Messiah who is about to die. He is anointed, paradoxically, for his death—which, in Johannine terms, is his "glorification."

The act of devotion by Mary is heightened by its contrast with Judas (vv. 4–6). What Mary did was objected to on pragmatic, calculating grounds by Judas. The fourth evangelist has come to believe that Judas is by now the instrument of Satan and that his wickedness is limitless. Two contrasting persons, Judas and Mary, are depicted here; two discrepant values are at work. Mary said nothing but did something whose odor filled the house. (This reference is probably symbolic of devotion to Jesus filling the earth.) Judas uttered his practical-sounding criticism. But his later action shows his central commitment to be divergent from that of Jesus—whose supreme value Mary genuinely grasped. Judas had his purposes, to which Jesus was instrumental. For Mary, Jesus was a value in himself; the worth of things was determined by their relation to him and his service.

The anointing by Mary is an act of spontaneous, uncalculating devotion. It is a reminder that there are things (or at least, by the ultimate standard, there is one thing) of such value that when they are found, the appropriate thing to do is to "sell all" for their sake. We maintain a cautious, controlled devotion to Christ—it stays in our hands and is not excessive. We strike a balance, a calculated less and more. It is part of the grip of self-centeredness that we do not lose ourselves. Love, by contrast, is a spendthrift. Devotion enjoys its moments of splendid extravagance. "Truly I say to you, this poor widow has put in more than all those who are contributing to the treasury. . . . For she has put in everything she had, her whole living" (Mark 12:43–44). For the most part, we occupy a middle range of experience, unacquainted with any end for which nothing is too good. Jesus, in the crisis of the kingdom, did not commend prudence. "When you give alms, do not let your left hand know what your right hand is doing" (Matt. 6:3). "Do good and lend, expecting nothing in return" (Luke 6:35). "The kingdom of heaven is like a merchant in search of fine pearls, who on finding one pearl of great value, went and sold all that he had and bought it" (Matt. 13:45).

Devotion arises out of the overwhelming awareness that someone else matters. Someone else matters to me more than I matter to myself. Someone else matters supremely.

Love can appropriately be expressed by an impractical, uncalculating act. In devotion, no one needs to fear being a fool—if it is for Christ's sake. Our tame, uninteresting religious communities badly need a holy recklessness, a divine folly. We might reckon the congregational life of a year against this pericope and ask whether it is dominated by the words of Judas or the act of Mary. This story is told to recall an act—an act unaccompanied by interpreting words. It was moved by an affection too big, too deeply felt for explanation. Something was offered. Something was given. Nothing was said. But the act was expressive all the same.

These readings for Monday in Holy Week bring before us important figures by which Christ has been apprehended—the suffering servant, the surpassing high priest and sacrifice, the Messiah anointed for his death/glory. The one reality of Christ—who he is, what he has done, what he means now for the experience of faith, the new situation for man he has brought into being—is so rich that many vocabularies, images, and forms of thought have been pressed into duty to express its meaning. The center of it all (most apparent in the events that center on the cross) is God's provision of an access to himself for estranged mankind—an access in which he is glorified and man is fulfilled.

Tuesday in Holy Week

Lutheran	*Roman Catholic*	*Episcopal*	*Presbyterian and UCC*
Isa. 49:1–6	Isa. 49:1–6	Isa. 49:1–9*a*	Isa. 42:1–9
1 Cor. 1:18–25		1 Cor. 1:18–31	1 Tim. 6:11–16
John 12:20–36	John 13:21–33, 36–38	John 12:37–38, 42–50	John 12:37–50

EXEGESIS

First Lesson: Isa. 49:1–6. This passage continues the series of "servant songs" from Second Isaiah. Some general comments on the servant material can be found in the introduction to the First Lesson for Monday.

The focus throughout this song is the vocation of the servant. Again he understands himself primarily through his verbal facility (v. 2*a*). He already hints that his appearance is genuinely deceptive of his ability (v. 2*b*).

He is ambivalent about the role already assigned to him from his mother's womb (v. 1). He has despaired about his success in the past (v. 4). But he has received a new call (v. 5), a higher commission. He will be a light to the nations. (Here the servant returns to a theme already at the center of his conception of his role as set forth in the first song.)

Second Lesson: 1 Cor. 1:18–25. Pauline thought is highly personalized. When Paul's position and authority are not threatened, he can be open and expansive. But when Paul is challenged, he comes on the strongest. The text before us is a case where Paul perceives his ministry and distinctive emphasis as being threatened by other Christian workers who have visited the Corinthians.

His argument is pitched basically against his opponents. They are advocates of miracles (Jews) and wisdom (Greeks). These he strongly attacks while he praises his own proclamation of Christ, the same Christ who was nailed to a cross.

Why exactly is Paul's proclamation to be preferred? One of the insinuations he makes is that since the wise men of this world are mortal, their wisdom cannot be significant. He chooses an episodic OT reference against the wise and develops it into a general program on the part of God (v. 21). In part he here prepares a base for those *via negativa* theologians who were to come later in the history of the church. The text is often cited in favor of Christian anti-intellectualism.

Of course this is all polemic. One is in fact only impressed by it if he imagines that Paul would not have to prove his own case. How does it happen that Paul has special access to the truth? What precisely is he pushing? An answer is not contained in this text. One needs to move forward to 2:4 to hear Paul pitting his proclamation against his opponents. "My speech and preaching was not with persuasive words of wisdom, but with a demonstration of the spirit and power." That is, Paul pits against the cerebral and spectacular positions of his opponents an energizing gospel which touches the lives of the offscouring of the world. It does not need proof. It is its own proof.

Gospel: John 12:20–36. This section from the Gospel of John shows Jesus in the process of coming to terms with his own death. The text itself does not have a complete symmetry. The Greeks introduced in v. 20 drop from view, and the section from v. 23 on seems to be played out before a crowd.

The Jesus of the Gospel of John can be characterized as "untouchable power." Throughout the narrative one has the sense that Jesus is so powerful that no one could do anything to him against his will. No, more. What happens to him must *be* his will. But how will the evangelist bring this "untouchable power" under the control of and make it subordinate to the initiative of the established religious and political leadership? A Jesus who was not nailed to the cross would not be the historical Jesus.

This section makes that transition. It begins softly. "The hour has come for the Son of man to be glorified" (v. 23). Good news. Only in the next verse is the note of death introduced, and even there perhaps only as a metaphor. That it is not simply a metaphor becomes clearer in v. 25. A more general saying about preservation of self (Mark 8:35 pars.) is used here to prepare for Jesus' death and transfer to another world.

V. 27 makes the sharpest possible contrast between Jesus and ordinary people. Unlike the parallel passage in Mark 14:34–36, where Jesus would like to escape his fate, here Jesus welcomes this fate with open arms and shows nothing of the all-too-human response of the Jesus of the synoptic gospels. In sure and certain expectation of approval, Jesus calls on God to verify his judgment. God responds with an instant theophany. (Note the contrast to the baptism of Jesus or even the transfiguration.) Jesus is anxious to point out that he certainly did not need a theophany. It was for the sake of the crowd.

Vv. 31–32 have ties with a gnostic view of the world. The irony is that in precisely that act in which the world understands itself to be judging Jesus, it is itself being judged. The ruler of the world will be cast out. Jesus himself will be raised up from the world. And he will draw all people to him. This kind of mythological picture is repeated in various gnostic systems (see Hans Jonas, *The Gnostic Religion* [Boston: Beacon Press, 1963]). The function of the redeemer is to free people from a world in which they find themselves prisoners. He will depart the earth and draw them after him. The particular genius of John was that he was able to connect this going up with the crucifixion of Jesus. This view of the function of Jesus has prevailed in Christendom for most of its history. Its relation to messianism is problematic.

The author must have sensed that conflict too, for he has the people raise a messianic objection in v. 34. Once the messiah had arrived, the rule of God would be established. How could the "lifting up of the Son of man" relate to that? John depicts Jesus as avoiding the question with a simile about light (vv. 35–36). The meaning in this context seems to be, "If you comprehended what I say you wouldn't ask questions like that."

So the death of Jesus is intended. The event works itself out within the world because Jesus appears as a dangerous madman to the world. Crucifixion is an appropriate end for a madman. The "bearer of subversive wisdom" becomes an "ultimate victim." (See Susan Sontag's "Approaching Artaud," *New Yorker*, 19 May 1973, p. 74 for an excellent description of the gnostic type.)

But in the plan and purpose of God the death of Jesus is his "way out" (exodus) and a way out for his people. In judging Jesus, the world judges itself. In thinking to destroy him, it accomplishes the purposes of God. And hence Jesus in the view of John retains his power, allowing himself to be touched only because now it is necessary for the culmination of his entire mission.

HOMILETICAL INTERPRETATION

In the song which is today's OT reading, the servant himself is the speaker. He explains to the world his credentials and his vocation.

A universal, missionary task was implicit in the calling of Israel. That task had been refused or neglected, and it appeared to have failed. But at this point in the community's history, the task falls to the servant, as true Israel. He is to give the law of God to the whole world. His message is addressed to distant Gentile nations, to those across the sea. The message concerns them. The servant claims no right to rule over the nations. It is his task to speak the news of universal redemption, to carry out his mission so that "redemption may reach to the ends of the earth."

The servant has been prepared in secret for his great work. He has been made ready "in the shadow of God's hand"—like a sharp sword in God's sheath or a polished arrow in God's quiver. The most important parts of God's work for us are hidden from us and from public knowledge. The ministry which will make God's glory manifest to all is prepared in secret. "Solitude is a great school of eloquence" (George Adam Smith). This hidden, solitary work provides a concentration of purpose without which public ministry lacks authority and staying power.

The purpose of the servant is that the Lord will be glorified. The outgoing presence of God in his creation must be recognized and reflected in all. The glory of the Lord is shown in the servant himself (v. 3), through the servant in bringing Israel back to God (v. 5), and through Israel in all the world (v. 6). The missionary task of Israel was apparently ended with the exile. "I have labored in vain. I have spent my strength for nothing and vanity." How could a weak and captive nation evidence God's glory among the people of the earth? But in this moment of discouragement, the prophet's vision builds. He looks to the Lord for right and recompense. "The missionary note gathers momentum out of the very chaos which has befallen the more modestly conceived plan of salvation" (Ulrich Simon).

This OT conviction has a later history. In Acts 13:47, when provincially-minded early believers opposed a wider witness, Paul and Barnabas cited this very passage in support of carrying the Christian mission to the Gentiles.

The servant's conception of himself as one who is to bear witness to God's redemption is carried on in the Second Lesson. The voice is Paul's.

The historical situation is different. But the prophetic task shows a deep continuity in the biblical community.

In the opening of the first Corinthian letter, Paul sets in the most radical form the opposition between God's actual way and man's expectations. He probably is replying to a faction whose watchword was "wisdom." For Paul (and for the early Christian community) what had happened in the life, death, and resurrection of Jesus Christ, in the revelation of his present lordship, in the coming of the Spirit, and in the summoning of a new community in Christ was—in its sweep, power, and effects—manifestly a work of God. Paul summarizes this divine activity by citing the most paradoxical, the most difficult, the most scandalous, and yet the most basic element: Christ crucified. When the Creator took action to show his wisdom and power and to restore his sinful world, he acted through (of all the unlikely things!) a man on a cross!

Paul does not argue this point. He preached it. It is for him a given fact of faith and community. It is his gospel.

He sets it over against the expectations of the religion of his time. The Jewish community, with its nonspeculative character, wanted a sign of God acting in power, vindicating his promise to his people. A crucified messiah was a contradiction in terms, a sign of God's weakness and defeat. The Greeks (the thoughtful non-Jewish world is probably meant) for their part sought wisdom. They had a sophisticated sense of what godlike propriety required—god as a cosmic principle; god as the presupposition, inspiration, goal, and guarantor of the human quest. A god made known in a cross violated the sensibilities of the Greek. Thus *man* —as seen in these two differing, yet serious, articulate groups—demonstrates the incompatibility of his ways and God's. When confronted by God making himself known in Christ, man's most religious and most refined expectations reject God. Man expects too little. He identifies his needs, but he does not know their true depth and character. Man on his own is demonstrated to be *against* God.

Yet the man on a cross ("Christ as having been crucified," v. 23) is God's true wisdom and power. God declares his wisdom through what looks like folly to men. God declares his power through what looks like weakness to men. But God's wisdom ultimately transcends man's shortsighted expectation; his power to save actually works through Christ and his cross. Man is looking so hard for something of his own devising that he cannot see the truth of God or accept the deliverance of God as they must be apprehended—on God's terms.

Confrontation with Christ crucified unites both Jew and Greek in rejection ("folly to those who are perishing"). But at the same time it creates a new unity among "those who are called, both Jews and Greeks." Here is a new center for true life—a life united with God and bridging the deepest religious cleavage within the human community. This new life looks at the man on a cross, embraces the paradox, abandons its own ideas of what God must do in order to be truly God, and of the cross says: "Here is God's wisdom. Here is God's power. Both are beyond our conceiving. Yet their very contradictoriness judges and reestablishes our communion with the transcendent God in action."

The church today is looking for its proper relationship to its society. Old patterns of communication have broken down. Common assumptions are under question. Social movements and new ideas seem to have thrown the church on the defensive. The gospel is being asked to respond to initiatives which lie outside the faith community. Those who preach a gospel of a man on a cross dare not be arrogant. The cross chastens its own proclaimers. Much of today's human wisdom that calls received opinions and customs into question is valuable and needed. It may be a manifestation of God's wisdom, addressed to the complacent community of faith. That is a biblical emphasis—but presumably it would be preached from other texts. This great Pauline passage is a reminder that the church's vindication comes not by meeting the expectations of others but by remaining loyal to its own message, its own Lord, and the task of proclamation. Christ crucified authenticates his own work. Man in every age is hungry not for a reflection of his own presuppositions, but for the concrete reality of God in saving action made known through credible witnesses.

To turn to the Gospel passage for today, some Greeks (probably God-fearer Gentiles in Jerusalem for the religious festival) ask to see Jesus. They then disappear from the story. They seem to have been brought on the scene to introduce Jesus' saying in vv. 23–26. Yet, in the mind of the author—who loves double or multiple meanings—this simple incident may symbolize the coming world mission of Christianity in which, through apostolic witness, the Gentiles would in fact see Jesus. (The remark "the world has gone after him" in v. 19 and the reference to universal salvation in v. 32 support the suggestion that such a wider meaning may be intended.)

Jesus speaks first of the coming of his "hour." Indeed, the passage sustains this theme: "The hour has come for the Son of man to be glorified" (v. 23). "And what shall I say, 'Father, save me from this hour'? No, for this purpose I have come to this hour" (v. 27). This solemn motif runs through the Fourth Gospel from the first miracle (2:4), through an abortive attempt at arrest (7:30), to the moments before the Passover observance in the upper room (13:1) and the opening of the great prayer (17:1). This term, Jesus' "hour," indicates the sense of divine purpose that underlies Jesus' mission. It is the "hour" of crucifixion, resurrection, and return to the Father which is the climax of Jesus' life as the evangelist sees it. The "hour" is connected with "glory" in vv. 23 and 27 and in 17:1. Yet the references become more numerous and more weighted in the setting of the passion narratives. This is the paradox of Jesus' life and death in the Fourth Gospel. Jesus comes from the Father; he is to bear witness to the Father and to do the will of the one who sent him; and he is to return to the Father. He glorifies the Father, and the Father glorifies him. Yet this divine mission leads to death. On the cross Jesus cries, as he dies, "Finished!" (19:30). The death is not the defeat of the "glorification." It is not the failure of the "hour." Rather, it is conceived in John as the achievement of the appointed "hour," as one episode in the "glorification." The way to the throne of glory was through death.

In vv. 24–26, the model of Jesus—his "hour," his death/glory—is connected with a way of life. It is something Jesus shares with others. "If any one serves me, he must follow me." What Jesus did is a paradigm of fulfilled and productive life. The seed, Jesus says, must fall into the ground and "die." It leaves our observation and control and is given to the mysterious, hidden forces of the earth. Unless it does, where we have one seed, we shall always have just that one seed. But if it "dies," it brings forth "much fruit." By analogy, Jesus says, if life is clutched and held, it is lost. If we are willing to venture, to accept life as a gift and use it for its Giver and for others, to let it go, it is kept. When such a role is accepted, it is not carried out alone; it is shared by another: "Where I am, there shall my servant be also."

One of the Johannine emphases that unite these themes is this: Jesus' own death was "the appointed means of freeing the work of Christ from its necessary limitations and making it available for all the world" (E. F.

Scott). He was like a seed which fell into the earth and died as a means to productivity. The universal Savior was first the crucified Jesus. He is reported in John (who finds the prayer in Gethsemane incompatible with his view of Jesus) as not asking to be saved from his "hour." It was, in fact, the purpose for which he had come (v. 27). It was the glorification of the Father (vv. 28 f.). It was the judgment of the world and the casting down of Satan (v. 31). It was the manifestation of the world's redeemer, the light to which all should be attracted (vv. 35–36). This universalization is spoken of as being "lifted up" (v. 32). The expression is another of John's multiple meanings (he has used it in 3:14 f. of a "lifting up" of Jesus for salvation and in 8:28 of a "lifting up" for judgment). It refers to Jesus' crucifixion (a "lifting up from the earth" in a starkly literal sense), and at the same time it refers to his ascension or return to the Father (the final "lifting up"). Its terminological background is complex, as the exegetical comments have suggested. But there is probably here some echo of Isa. 52:13: "Behold my servant . . . shall be exalted and lifted up." The paradox of suffering and glory–of individual rejection and salvation for the many–is present in this prophetic passage. As the one "lifted up," Jesus can draw "all men" to himself. He will not be the rabbi from Nazareth. His significance will be unbounded, universally accessible, cosmic.

The NT does not deal with universality and particularity as a problem in abstract thought. But as the literature of a community which proclaimed a specific, historical personage as the focus of a faith which claimed a world hearing, the issue is recognized. Material for dealing with it pervades every variety of NT thought. This Gospel pericope (which contains the last words in Jesus' public ministry as recounted in John) suggests that this one life (and death) could make a difference for the situation of mankind because it was the life of one who came forth from the Father, an expression of his eternal creative purpose, and of one who lived for the Father's glory and the winning of others, and who was faithful even to his appointed "hour."

Wednesday in Holy Week

Lutheran	*Roman Catholic*	*Episcopal*	*Presbyterian and UCC*
Isa. 50:4–9*a*	Isa. 50:4–9*a*	Isa. 50:4–9*a*	Isa. 52:13–53:12
Rom. 5:6–11		Heb. 9:11–15, 24–28	Rom. 5:6–11
Matt. 26:14–25	Matt. 26:14–25	John 13:21–35 (Matt. 26:1–5, 14–25)	John 12:37–50

EXEGESIS

First Lesson: Isa. 50:4–9a. Again the First Lesson resumes the servant songs, and introductory material on the series of songs can be found in the exegesis for Monday.

A new theme is sounded in this, the third of the servant songs. After reviewing once again with appreciation his own gifts as a teacher and as a counselor for others, the servant notes that God is developing in him a new gift, that of hearing (v. 4)—a role of the pupil.

The servant's new learning is the result not of scholarly reflection but of severe rejection. He endures punishment which he describes in vv. 5 and 6. He does not avoid this punishment and is able to endure it because of his confidence that the Lord is supporting him.

His attitude seems to show a hardening as a result of his experience. Instead of singing songs of grandeur and world mission, the servant digs in for bad times. The one who says, "I have set my face like flint" (NEB), does not call up the image of a teacher or orator. Rather, the chiseled features of an embattled warrior come to mind. He takes his stand against all comers, awaiting the sure vindication at the hand of the Lord.

Second Lesson: Rom. 5:6–11. Here we find Paul working within a very tight system. Christ, a righteous man, died for us, the unrighteous, at that time when we had no power to justify ourselves. Since Paul connects Jesus intimately with God, he takes this to be a sign of God's love for us (v. 8).

The backdrop for this view is the righteousness of God conceived as a quality which prevents him from having contact with unrighteous people.

The act of Jesus, or better, of God in Jesus, makes all who are attached to him righteous. Hence while he can refer to them as former sinners (v. 8), that would not be a proper description after their justification (since they and God are now *just*).

In the language of Paul, the act of God in Jesus does not only have past ramifications in that it has created sinless (justified) people. It also means two additional benefits which are outlined in vv. 10 and 11. V. 10 is an affirmation that the difficult act was the act of justification. If God was able to accomplish that, then he certainly will have no trouble saving man from death. Further, this new status of being reconciled to God brings a general state of good feeling, exultation, which characterizes the believer's present existence in Christ. He need no longer suffer from any kind of fear.

Gospel: Matt. 26:14–25. In dramatic analysis, a distinction is made between the denouement of the play and the climax. The denouement is that point where an action is taken from which the rest of the play runs to its inexorable end. The Gospel for this day is such a story.

It is a concise dramatic unit. Later scenes in the drama will have more characters, more action, even more obvious meaning. But in this encounter we are presented with the inner fragmentation of the community of Jesus.

Vv. 14–16 introduce a member of Jesus' inner circle, Judas, in the unlikely company of the chief priests. We soon learn that he has gone to them to see whether he can get something out of betraying Jesus to them. According to Matthew, the contract was made, and Judas began to look for a chance to meet it.

Vv. 17–19 introduce the other main character in the scene, Jesus. He is in the process of making arrangements for the Passover celebration. That Matthew has no interest in the scene itself other than to make the Passover celebration possible is evident from his failure to include the element of mystery in the arrangements present in Mark 14:12–16. This purpose is served simply by bringing Jesus and Judas together.

Vv. 20–25 are the heart of the scene. It is set simply, Jesus sitting with the twelve disciples. No incidental detail is included. Rather the action moves directly to the point of the scene: a confrontation of the betrayer. It must have been an electric moment when Jesus suddenly shifted the conversation during the meal and said, "One of you will betray me."

The rest of the pericope revolves around the disciples' response to this accusation. They were deeply hurt. And the response of each was (literally), "Certainly not I, Lord?" It was a question which was really saying, "How could you possibly even suspect me of such a thing?"

Jesus makes a double response. The first, v. 23, designates the betrayer as one who has dipped his hand into the common bowl with Jesus. This has been understood, in paintings for example, as a simultaneous dipping. Most translations, however, take it as a general reference to those at the meal, pointing up specifically that one who has shared so closely with Jesus is now to be the agent of his destruction. His second response represents Jesus' interpretation of the betrayal. On the one hand the betrayer has done nothing, because it has already been determined in advance ("as it is written") that there is a certain path that Jesus has to follow. In spite of that, however, full responsibility for betrayal rests upon the betrayer. In this view, determinism does not eliminate personal responsibility.

The pressure of the occasion builds to its own climax. Judas is driven to ask, "Certainly you don't mean me, Rabbi?" and in classic understatement Jesus says, "You said it."

Jesus suffers the worst that can be suffered, betrayal by friends. But as is so commonly asserted in the theology of the passion narrative, even the worst that friends (or enemies) can do will not frustrate the purposes of God in Jesus.

HOMILETICAL INTERPRETATION

In this lesson from Second Isaiah, the servant speaks for himself; we hear his own account of his role and mission. The song is more personal and individualized than are the earlier ones of the series.

V. 4 presents the theme of the interdependence of speaking and listening. The servant is to use that most fragile, yet most powerful and deeply human medium: the spoken word. He is to "sustain with a word him that is weary." For such a ministry, God must endow him with gifts of utterance. But the emphasis of the servant is not on his gifts of speech, but on his role as a listener. The servant speaks as one who has been spoken to. Each day begins with listening to the voice of God. The first task of the Christian community or the individual believer is to listen. The beginning of salvation is in listening. "Faith comes by hearing." The beginning of worship, prayer, obedience, service, community is also in listening. We have nothing to say until in the depths of our own life we have first heard. The authority for proclamation lies in a personal, attentive communion with God. The speaking is public—in and for the community—but the preparation is a private, unshared listening.

Vv. 5 and 6 indicate the struggle of one who hears and speaks faithfully—and is rejected and made a mockery. Prophets, in the biblical succession, have never had an easy time of it. Suffering for one's own words, for the God-given word, for the Word's sake is all too familiar. Jesus' lament, "O Jerusalem, Jerusalem, killing the prophets and stoning those who are sent to you," has its thousand echoes. Those who tell new truth or remind of forgotten truth tend to uncover the distortion or expose the complacency of the community. Troublers of Israel are seldom thanked for their pains.

Vv. 7–9 speak of the vindication and confidence of the servant. The community may be uncomprehending. The task of speaking in God's name can bring about a desolating isolation—even from the community the prophet loves and for whose sake he is called, and whose deepest and most precious secrets he announces. But the ultimate help and advocacy does not come from the community, but from God. The confidence in God can bring steadiness and determination when all other supports have given way: "I have set my face like a flint, and I know that I shall not be put to shame; he who vindicates me is near."

Vv. 8 and 9 are a series of questions, asking who can stand against or accuse the one who knows his life and purpose to be rooted in God. Paul, in Rom. 8:33, adapts these questions to speak not of the exceptional, courageous prophet, but of the secure standing and forgiveness which are assured to every Christian believer. The true Servant suffered. The people in him may share the misunderstanding and rejection as they bear witness to God's truth. But they share the sense of vindication —secured in the triumph of the Servant, Jesus Christ, and the solidarity of his people in him.

The theme of God's vindication of his chosen ones continues in the Second Lesson for today. The passage ends, "We rejoice in God through our Lord Jesus Christ, through whom we have now received our reconciliation" (v. 11). The servant's confident tone is present, but a crucial factor is now added in the phrase "through Jesus Christ our Lord."

The appointed passage from Romans contains a forceful statement of the link between the love of God and the death of Christ. "God shows his love for us in that while we were yet sinners Christ died for us" (v. 8). It was an extraordinary feature of early Christian thought (verified in subsequent generations of faith) that the death of Christ is connected with the love of God. Christ's crucifixion is, from one angle of vision, the very sort of event that makes us question the character of God and his providential governance. The best of men endures the worst ignominy and the cruelest death. Why, if God is a God of love, did he allow such a thing to happen? The event might have made cynics of the followers of Jesus. God, they might have concluded, was dead, napping, powerless, malign, indifferent . . .

But Christian faith saw (and sees) in the cross of Christ a demonstration of the love of God. It was not evidence of the pointlessness and moral disorder of the world. It was not a merciful Jesus appeasing an angry Father. Rather, it was a revelation of what God is like: the one who loves, who loves sacrificially, who loves to the uttermost. For Christian faith, Christ's character and acts—culminating in his cross—are God's character and acts. Christ's work is God's work. "God shows his love in that Christ died for us."

But the death of Christ was not simply a demonstration of the love of God. "Love cannot be conceived of as doing anything gratuitously, merely to show its own depth" (J. McLeod Campbell). God acted to meet a genuine need. The condition of man, for whose sake Christ died, was in Paul's estimate desperate. He indicates it in this pericope by several terms: "helpless" (v. 6), "wicked" (v. 6, NEB), "sinners" (v. 8), "enemies" (v. 10). Such terms are stronger than a mere statement that man is weak, pitiable, and foolish. They suggest man as rebel, as opponent of God. Man has organized his own life—individual and corporate—in defiance of the order and love of the Creator.

Paul proclaims that God's love—taking action in Christ—overcame this enmity. Paul contrasts this love of God for his enemies (an unmotivated love, springing from God's own character) with the kinds of self-sacrifice which may appear in human relationships. He is not contrasting good love (God's) with corrupt love (man's). Perhaps he started to do that in v. 7 and then had second thoughts. He does not belittle human love, but he does indicate that it provides no real measure for the kind of love we know in God's reconciling act. There would be some accounting for loving the lovable; but God loves—and Christ died for—sinners.

This love was effective. When Paul speaks of what has been done about sin, several complementary terms are again used to describe one infinitely rich reality. We are "justified" (v. 9), "reconciled" (vv. 10, 11), and we shall be "saved" (vv. 9, 10). These are metaphors from common experience called into service to express the meaning of God's act in Christ. A just court declares a guilty person righteous—"justification." Persons at odds over a bargain are brought together—"reconciliation." One with an apparently incurable disease is given health—"salvation." Each of these images has become, in the generations of theological in-talk, a technical term—abstract and polemic. But originally each was a freshly grasped image expressing something of what life in Christ is like. It is like being guilty and yet declared just, like being restored to a relation basic to one's very being, like being made whole from a deadly illness. When these terms are seen pictorially again, they take on life; they speak from faith to faith; they lend themselves to proclamation.

These terms and this experience are known from within. (Note the recurrent "we" in this section of Romans. Paul writes out of and for a community of shared life, history, experience, and vocabulary.) A new life and fellowship has been created within the messianic order. Love and forgiveness prevail for those who know they do. All that needs to be done or can be done about sin has been done. The Messiah who once died (a thing so difficult to conceive!) now lives (a thing given in the life of faith and community). Therefore a Christian faces the present and the future with confidence and joy.

The passage appointed for today's Gospel is dominated by Judas and his act of betrayal. The evangelists report this event with a sense of shock: "He who has dipped his hand in the dish with me will betray me" (v. 23). The fact that Jesus was given over into the hands of his enemies by one of his close group of disciples haunted those who told the story.

But when it came to an explanation of Judas, the early church gave no satisfactory account. Vv. 14–16 tell of Judas agreeing to betray Jesus for a payment of money. But Matthew probably dwells on the money feature of the story because of its correlation with what he takes to be the prophecy of Zech. 11:12. He does little to suggest that the betrayal was done expressly for the sake of money.

The fact is that we ask questions out of psychological interests which the gospel writers did not entertain. They wrote for their own purposes, and they do not give material out of which psychological inquiry can usefully be followed. The evangelists are baffled. Judas cannot be explained in human terms; the writers fall back on Satan. The external facts must be told, for without them something necessary to the actual story is left out. But Judas, in the gospels, fits into no meaningful historical context. William Barclay has commented: "We may well feel that Judas Iscariot is the supreme enigma of the New Testament."

Modern reconstructions of the life of Jesus seek to deal more fully with Judas. The presence of conflict within Jesus' intimate company is, for artistic purposes, irresistible. It is often commented that no one could act so wickedly unless he was more than ordinarily able as well as more than ordinarily flawed. Judas has been presented as very clever—as an intellectual, a political or religious visionary, one who means by his betrayal to force Jesus to act boldly as king, one who is horrified by the results of his own acts. Yet all such constructions multiply conjecture. Whatever role is given to Judas is a function of the general conception an author has of Jesus and his mission. Judas cannot seize control of the story.

The gospels leave us with the brute, almost unassimilable fact that one who had been close to Jesus could yet betray him. Jesus involved his disciples deeply in his ministry. He once said to them, "He who hears you hears me, and he who rejects you rejects me" (Luke 10:16). The company of the chosen followers who had cast out demons, who had tread on serpents, who had proclaimed the kingdom, who had shared in Jesus' mighty words and acts, contained one failure.

Perhaps the homiletical point is that we dare not presume. We may ask, "Lord, is it I?" We are capable of betraying the best we know and destroying what we love. Good motives (as we judge ourselves) cannot preserve us from blunders. Past success cannot assure us that we know what is best in new situations. We see ourselves indulgently. We build our self-deceptions on one another. The point of Judas for a preacher is not, of course, that we are all Judases at heart or that we are always evil and incapable of goodness and altruism. Apparently right to the end, the other disciples thought well of Judas—probably with adequate reason. Rather, the point is that life is difficult and we are vulnerable—and never more so than when we forget it. When we are quite sure that the will of God is our will and that by our initiative we can put it into effect, we are in peril.

Judas is a mystery. Evil is a mystery. We are mysteries to ourselves. We take due warning. But the Judas story is retold in Holy Week as part of the good news of redemption. It represents a massive, inexplicable presence of evil in close association with the events of redemption. But the purpose of God prevailed over the worst that discreative forces could do. We only know of Judas because his name stands forever linked with Jesus. The story is one of salvation in Christ Jesus—in which Judas figures. Intended by no one and guessed by no one, the passion events play out the drama in which one man died for Judas—and for everyman.

Maundy Thursday

Lutheran	*Roman Catholic*	*Episcopal*	*Presbyterian and UCC*
Jer. 31:31–34	Exod. 12:1–8, 11–14	Exod. 12:1–14*a*	Num. 9:1–3, 11–12
Heb. 10:15–39	1 Cor. 11:23–26	1 Cor. 11:23–26	1 Cor. 5:6–8
Luke 22:7–20	John 13:1–15	Luke 22:14–30 (John 13:1–15)	Mark 14:12–26

EXEGESIS

First Lesson: Jer. 31:31–34. The idea of a new covenant did not make its first appearance in the first century A.D. In the mind of the prophet Jeremiah it was a viable way out of Judah's difficulties in the sixth century B.C. Much of his prophecy in this section before us is one that uses covenantal language.

A recent scholarly work has argued persuasively that Jeremiah's teaching concerning a new covenant grew out of a negative anthropology (see "The New Covenant in Jeremiah 31:31–34 and Its Place in the Covenant-Treaty Tradition of Israel and the Ancient Near East" [Ph.D. diss., Dropsie College, 1971] by Frank Seilhamer of the Hamma School of Theology). This work indicates that Jeremiah wanted God to make an order of things in which people would not find it possible to disobey the law. Teaching would no longer be required. Social advantage and disadvantage would disappear.

This new covenant is different from that which Christians understood to have been established in Jesus. It rather is comparable with the pre-

Christian descriptions which anticipate the age of the messiah, which is here thought of in covenantal categories.

The language of the Spirit depicts an internal placement of the wishes and purposes of God. From this feature of Jeremiah's thought, it is easy to establish an identification with the period of the early church—a period depicted as an age of the Spirit.

What Jeremiah does fervently wish for is a new beginning—a beginning which would be spared the uncertainties of institutional communications of goodness and the frailty of people. His vision may sound like a kind of messianic overkill. But it grows out of a thoroughgoing critique of past failure and a realization that partial renewal will not do.

Second Lesson: Heb. 10:15–39. Hebrew's use of the new covenant material from Jeremiah is very interesting in the light of the Seilhamer thesis that Jeremiah's prediction of a new covenant grew out of a very negative anthropology. Jeremiah wanted to make it impossible for people to sin again by the direct inscription of the Torah upon their hearts. It is one thing to live as a prophet and predict for the future. It is quite another to write as one who shares an equally judgmental view of people but who lives in the period after this new covenant has been established.

The function the new covenant plays for the author of Hebrews can be indicated by comparison with the actions of a mother who finds her child's room messy. She vows that she will clean the room but that if the child ever gets the room dirty again she will throw the child out of the house. It is a question whether the mother did the child a favor by cleaning the room if she was going to set such stringent measures thereafter.

A new stringency seems to be a concomitant of this internalized covenant. The author appears to be encountering some waning of participation in the assemblies (v. 25). His is a double response. First he warns his hearers how stern God is (vv. 26–31). He makes it clear that this stern God will judge in the future. Then he calls to mind the glorious past of the group, when under circumstances of persecution they bore up bravely (vv. 32–35). But the problem he now faces is that internal discipline and vigilance are best supported by external persecution. In a period when things are more relaxed, people are more likely to relax. But relaxation works against the loyalty that the author seems to identify with righteousness. Hence he ends with a quotation from Hab. 2:3–4 which predicts the near fruition of a vision (in the Hebrew) or the Lord (in the Greek).

If people do not experience a stringency in their actual existence, it can be brought in by predictions of the future. Instead of this stern attitude, the author might have allowed the developing experience of the group to shape actual pastoral theology and practice. And he might have modified his understanding of the new covenant accordingly.

Gospel: Luke 22:7–20. The broader context of this passage has been covered in the exegesis of the text for Passion Sunday. Here we will concentrate on the meal itself.

The first question to be sorted out is the extent of the text to be dealt with. Most modern translations relegate vv. 19*b* and 20 to the footnotes. While they are represented in the majority of manuscript traditions, the arguments against them are based upon their absence from a portion of the manuscript tradition and on the fact that it is much more understandable that they would have been added than that they would have been dropped. Their inclusion makes for a rather strange double cup ritual. The interpretation here will proceed on the assumption that the text ends with v. 19*a*, "This is my body."

The occasion of the meal is pointed up in v. 7. It is the ancient festival of Passover, a commemoration of that time when Israel had been delivered from Egypt. It is a festival of freedom and a commemoration of the establishment of the nation (one should note that neither of these ideas would make an occupying power comfortable). It is a pilgrim festival, when as many people as possible would want to be in Jerusalem. Vv. 8–13 tell of the arrangements that Jesus and his disciples made with considerable difficulty so that they would have a place to celebrate the Passover among the throngs of pilgrims in Jerusalem.

The words uttered by Jesus within the context of the meal are a solemn vow. He has looked forward to the common celebration of the Passover with his disciples. But the meal is the occasion for his announcement that it is the last time he will participate in the Passover until it is fulfilled in the kingdom of God. He repeats the words with a vow of abstinence over the wine. Finally he distributes broken bread with the strange comment, "This is my body."

What does it all mean? In the context of his understanding of his own life, Jesus is represented as coming to a turning point. He renounces participation in the Passover under the circumstances presently prevailing in the world. He renounces the drinking of wine, one of the standard vows in Judaism. Neither renunciation suggests that Jesus expected his sudden demise. He could get along without wine and could separate himself from participation in future community festivals. But his last word is more ominous and prophetic. Jesus' body would soon be broken. Using the bread as a symbol for his body meant that the disciples had some share in that.

HOMILETICAL INTERPRETATION

The great OT passage chosen for today's First Lesson speaks of the relationship between God and his people in terms of covenant. God dignifies the humanity he has made by calling persons into responsible relation with himself. "I will be their God and they will be my people."

The old covenant which had been entered into when God took his people by the hand and brought them out of Egypt was a covenant of loyalty to God expressed through legal conformity. The loyalty had been violated; the laws had been disobeyed.

But Jeremiah does not stop with the failure of the old covenant and the consequent judgment of God. He looks to the future—to a new era and a new covenant, and to new persons to live under it. The old covenant does not need to be renegotiated. Something qualitatively different needs to take its place. The new covenant which Jeremiah envisions is a gift. God speaks, promises, and acts. Note the expressions of divine initiative: "I will make . . ."; "I will put . . ."; "I will write . . ."; "I will be . . ."; "I will forgive . . ."; "I will remember no more." He who alone can do so forgets the sins of the past and does a new work.

The old covenant, as Jeremiah sees it, was principally defined in terms of regulations and lore to be imparted from person to person and from generation to generation. It was external, and it had a secondhand quality as it was communicated. The new covenant, by contrast, would be inward. Knowledge of God would be given by God himself to each—from the least to the greatest. The firsthand awareness of God would not belong to a prophetic elite. By the knowledge of God, Jeremiah meant insight into the character of God (Jer. 9:24) and an inward reflection of that character in one's own personal qualities (see the characterization of Josiah in 22:16).

This prophecy speaks to the sense of transformation and newness within history. Humanity has often hungered for a new age and recognized that such an age would require new social arrangements and a new consciousness on the part of those who were to live in it. There is a widespread realization that in our own time we are living in one of the great periods of transformation in history. The eschatology of the Bible can give insight into the dynamics of moments of newness.

But this vision which has its partial analogues in the movements of history looks forward to the Christian revelation, the new era, the new creation, the new birth, the new heart. These things are real and present and celebrated as such in the Christian community. Yet in another sense they are unrealized; their presence is pledged. Our having them and our not having them define the character of Christian life.

This passage is appropriate for Maundy Thursday, for it is echoed in the Pauline account of the Lord's Supper. In 1 Cor. 11:25, Paul reports Jesus as saying, "This cup is the new covenant in my blood." This passage is an early theological interpretation of the Eucharist. The blood of Christ is the blood of the covenant (an expression based on Exod. 24:8) —the establishment of a new order of forgiveness and a new and perfect fellowship with God. The Christian Eucharist is a festival of the new age, a celebration of a new relation with God, an affirmation of a new community practicing a new style of life.

The portion of Hebrews which has been chosen as today's Second Lesson begins with a Christian citation of Jeremiah's prophecy of the new covenant. The Christian author applies the prophet's words to redemption in Christ. The new covenant is established. God's laws are written on believing hearts. Sins are forgotten.

Once this point is affirmed, the author turns to a practical exhortation based on it. Modern readers often have difficulty with the argument and the cultic references of Hebrews. But the religion and ethics of the book are generally clear, and, except for the rigorism, they can be appealing.

The material that follows "Therefore, brothers" is lengthy and full. But threads may be gathered for emphasis:

Let us draw near (vv. 19–22). Hebrews argues that Christ has acted as elder brother in a large family. He is the "firstborn," the "pioneer" (2:10; 12:2), the "forerunner on our behalf" (6:20). What Jesus did, in this representative capacity, makes a difference for the others in the family. The spirituality of Hebrews is derived from this central affirmation. Jesus entered the presence of God; he came in victory into the true holy place. The author seems to say: "The barriers are torn away. Draw near to God where Jesus has opened the way. Live near to God. Enter upon the access which has been won."

Hold fast your confession (vv. 23–29). The author implies that some Christians are falling into neglect or abandonment of their commitments. The early church was not a deeply established, diversified, historical community, patiently leading and teaching its members in Christian experience and responsibility. It was more like an elite corps, expecting little short of heroism from a hand-picked membership—and, to some extent, getting it. The early community was shocked with a terrible sense of betrayal by those who broke ranks. This passage represents one of the first attempts to deal with the problem of postbaptismal sin. It assumes that no second chance is possible; the repentance at conversion is one's only opportunity. If it were not, the decisiveness of that confession would be compromised. One cannot presume on God. Such an approach to the issue seems to us to have theological and pastoral inadequacies. But the church today tends to solve the matter of sin in Christian life by minimizing its importance. We seem to say, "Wasn't the rigorism and moralism of the early church unfortunate—allowing for one repentance, or at most for two. By the way, we don't have the problem." The author of Hebrews insists that the matter is of the utmost importance. He would be as shocked at our complacency as we are by his sternness.

Do not shrink back (vv. 38, 39). The author regards faith as a reaching forward (cf. 11:1–12:2, especially 11:13–16). All organic life grows by a form or principle of its own unfolding, and it comes to maturity unless it is damaged by an external force. The greatness and the misery of specifically human life is that we can fail to grow; we can refuse to grow. Throughout life, God stands, calling us into a future of his appointment. By our own act, we can shrink back and be "destroyed" (v. 39). This possibility is seen here as a test of faith. Reaching forward or drawing back are radical alternatives. To shrink back is evidence of doubt or unbelief. Faith is a dynamic force by which one who believes claims the future and lives by what is coming to be.

To turn to the account of the Lord's Supper in Luke's gospel, Jesus and his disciples secure a guest room where they observe the Passover. This feast had its special temple rites, but for most Jews it was a household observance. Jesus and his followers constituted a unit like a family, and Jesus in this domestic ceremony took the place of the father. The lamb is not mentioned. But the formalities which began and ended the meal and included the explanatory words of the head of the household are dwelt upon by the narrators. These are the parts which (through a development now hard to reconstruct) came together in the Christian Eucharist.

Two of Jesus' sayings (vv. 15 and 18) connect this Passover with the kingdom of God. Jesus renounced participation in the feast under present conditions; he looked towards its observance under new and transformed conditions. At the Passover the Jewish family prayers of blessing praised God for his acts of calling and redemption. They ended with a plea for the coming kingdom. From the time of his first preaching in Galilee, Jesus had presented himself and his mission as a fresh act of God—the fulfillment of the age, the drawing near of the kingdom. His teaching had spoken of this decisive movement of God; his miracles had been its compelling signs. At this Passover, did Jesus extend the recital of God's mighty acts in the emancipation from Egypt and the giving of the law so as to include his own inauguration of the kingdom? Whether or not he looked back over his own ministry, Jesus is recorded as anticipating the kingdom. The meal was connected with what God was about to do as well as with what he had done.

Probably Jesus did not, at the time, know fully what the next steps would be. The new age would in fact be brought about in a way that could not be anticipated. But Jesus knew that the God who had acted in his ancient people was acting anew. A climactic point had been reached in Jesus' own mission. This meal belonged to the ultimate kingdom, to God's next and decisive move.

The Christian Eucharist, at its most vital, cannot lose this sense of expectancy. It is an eschatological act. It connects the middle of history with the end.

In the early church, the Eucharist was a meal shared with the risen Christ (cf. Luke 24:30; Acts 1:4; 10:41; Rev. 3:20). It was a fellowship with the one who lived beyond death and who would come (1 Cor. 11:26). It was a participation, by the Holy Spirit, in the power of the coming age. In an early third-century liturgy, the baptismal Eucharist at Easter included a cup of milk and honey—symbolizing the promised land to which the baptized had been brought.

The death of Christ is, for the Christian church, now clearly incorporated in the Holy Communion. It is widely understood that the

Eucharist is a "showing forth the Lord's death." But the link that Jesus forged "on the night in which he was betrayed" between this meal and the final kingdom provides a permanent element in eucharistic faith and spirituality that is no less important. The Communion is a "showing forth the Lord's death *till he come*." It is a joyful celebration of a victory won. It is an eager anticipation of a victory pledged.

It may not be too much to say that eucharistic piety in the West, Catholic and Protestant, has not been very eucharistic. It has been dominated by the memorial of the cross rather than by the triumph of the resurrection and the glory of the kingdom. It has been Good Friday piety rather than Easter piety. It has been preoccupied with our sins and Jesus' passion.

Jesus himself desired to eat the Passover with his disciples before he suffered (v. 7). But at that Passover, with all of the realistic foreboding that doubtless suffused the event, Jesus looked beyond it. The context of his thought was the ultimate vindication and reign of God. The meal was a victory banquet celebrated in advance. That is what it still is.

Good Friday

Lutheran	*Roman Catholic*	*Episcopal*	*Presbyterian and UCC*
Isa. 52:13–53:12	Isa. 52:13–53:12	Isa. 52:13–53:12	Hos. 6:1–6
Heb. 9:15–22	Heb. 4:14–16; 5:7–9	Heb. 10:1–25	Rev. 5:6–14
John 18:1–19:42	John 18:1–19:42	John 18:1–19:37	Matt. 27:31–50

EXEGESIS

First Lesson: Isa. 52:13–53:12. The fourth and final servant song begins with a strong theme of vindication, the exaltation of the servant. This initial theme disappears until v. 10, when it reappears. In a sense, however, vindication dominates the entire song. The portion from 52:14 to 53:9 is historical reminiscence. It has none of the anguish of being in the middle of a time of trial which marks the third song (50:4–9). It looks back as at the end of a long ordeal.

The corporate-individual tension is reflected in 52:14, 15: "Time was when many were aghast at you my people; so now many nations recoil at the sight of him" (NEB). The language shifts from "my people" to "him." The experience of the servant can be paralleled with that of the nation, but they were not precisely the same.

The servant's discovery, which appears in this song, is that his life, his biography, was important in the plan and purpose of the Lord. In the earlier songs he had seen himself as a bringer of a message. By the third psalm he realized that there was a certain necessity in his suffering. But it was a kind of "degree in the school of hard knocks" which he would endure with fortitude.

In this final song, the servant is viewed differently. Instead of the earlier pictures of success and great progress through his ability as a spokesman (49:2; 50:4), he begins this song by looking back at the improbable and painful elements of the servant's life. Instead of the slightly grandiose "he named me from my mother's womb," he uses the leaner image of a scraggly plant in thirsty ground (53:2). Instead of his gifts (50:4), he cites his ugliness (53:3). No longer is the servant seen as an oracle or a messenger. His work is to bear the punishment of others. A key verse is 53:5: "But he was pierced for our transgressions, tortured for our iniquities; the chastisements he bore is health for us and by his scourging we are healed" (NEB). The mystery is not the fact that the servant took a punishment which should rightfully fall to others, but that his chastisement is health for others and his scourging is healing for others. For Second Isaiah it must have been a meaning born out of his experience. Health may (will?) be served through the suffering of an innocent.

Second Isaiah is neither sadist nor masochist. The servant is vindicated, given long life, a renewed reputation, position in the community. His giving is answered with the giving of God, a return to a rich and full life.

This song has played an important role in the interpretation of the death of Jesus. The Greek of this servant song has many terms in common with the passion narrative in the gospels. For instance, Isa. 53:12 is applied to the two men reported to have been crucified with Jesus (Luke 22:37). Eduard Lohse's *History of the Suffering and Death of Jesus Christ* (Philadelphia: Fortress Press, 1967) makes clear how the OT Scriptures shaped the telling of the passion story.

Researches into the formation of the passion narrative indicate that the servant material influenced the way in which the early church came to terms with the death of Jesus. The use of servant material in 1 Pet. 2:24, 25 and in Acts 8:32, 33 suggests this influence. But what general parallels bear out the idea that the suffering and death of Jesus were interpreted through the servant songs?

Three factors seem to have been significant: (1) Like the servant, Jesus possessed gifts. Jesus was a sensitive interpreter of the world of nature and human interaction in which he moved. He saw the activity and character of God manifested in that world. (2) Like the servant, Jesus took on a mission. In many ways it was less ambitious than the servant's mission. He did not seem to have the Gentiles in view except as he encountered them. He did not even seem to center on a reconstituted Israel. He went about doing good, using his powers of healing and teaching to touch those people with whom he came in contact. He gathered disciples around that mission. (3) Like the servant, Jesus suffered and, according to the testimony of his followers, was vindicated. The suffering did not seem to be his mission, but grew out of his mission.

When these three factors—gifts, mission, and suffering and vindication—are considered together, the career of the servant makes an appropriate model for making sense of Jesus.

Second Lesson: Heb. 9:15–22. The thought of Hebrews sometimes makes strange leaps and combines themes unexpectedly. The examination of these features sometimes brings the author's argument out more forcefully. In today's passage, the author uses the Greek word *diathēkē*, which means both "agreement" and "will" (as in last will and testament). When we think of *diathēkē* as "covenant" or "agreement," we think of the setting of certain rules by which two parties agree to govern their relations with one another. But when we think of a "will," we imagine some benefits that are distributed after the death of the maker of the will. By a play on words, the author moves from *diathēkē* as agreement (the Mosaic covenant) to *diathēkē* as will. A death seals the agreement; a death cancels the offenses under the old covenant; a death makes available the inheritance.

The passage builds to the final words, "Without the shedding of blood there is no forgiveness." The value to be gained is forgiveness. Forgiveness is obtained through the shedding of blood. This seems to stretch the sense of the OT, but it is possible to penetrate beyond the author's reasoning to what he is trying to say.

For him, sin is a terribly serious matter. In 10:26 he says, "If we willfully persist in sin after receiving the knowledge of the truth, no sacrifice for sin remains: only a terrifying expectation of judgment and a fierce fire which will consume God's enemies." Coming to terms with such a God cannot be a casual thing. Yet the blood of Jesus is effective.

The author seeks a little elbowroom between a stern God and a threatening death or fear of death. He carves out a narrow corridor of escape, established through Jesus' shedding of blood and maintained through a capacity to endure suffering (10:32–36). The one who created this way of escape himself suffered in accomplishing his work: "It was clearly fitting that God for whom and through whom all things exist should, in bringing many sons to glory, make the leader who delivers them perfect through suffering" (2:10).

This author can also interpret the death of Jesus as a blow at the devil, who has death at his command (2:14). Here he sees the liberation from the fear of death as an existential benefit of the death of Jesus.

The shedding of blood thus makes an appropriate connection between the Christian message and the OT themes which are the source of the typology of Hebrews. But the thought of Hebrews coheres around the theme of suffering. Suffering befalls Christians, but if they stand fast they will receive an ample reward. The thrust of Hebrews lets us understand the death of Jesus from within the world by substituting "without suffering there is no life" for the externally shaped "without the shedding of blood there is no forgiveness."

Gospel: John 18:1–19:42. This segment includes the entire passion narrative of the Gospel of John. Here there is no Gethsemane. That is true in two senses. First, the location of the action is not Gethsemane but a garden across the Kidron ravine. This is only one small indication that when we are in the Johannine passion narrative, we are on terrain that is for the most part unfamiliar to the synoptic gospels. But there is also no Gethsemane in the metaphorical sense of that word. There is no struggle.

The story of the arrest in 18:1–12 sounds something like an account of a country sheriff who has received the unpleasant assignment of arresting the local earl. The class differences between the two are great. The sheriff is only able to carry out his task because as soon as he enters the house, hat in hand, the earl takes over the operation and makes all arrangements for his own arrest. When the arresting soldiers come, Jesus steps forward and asks who they are looking for. Judas is present but does nothing to identify Jesus. Jesus remains untouchable power. If there are any lingering doubts, the awed collapse of the arresting company in v. 6 makes this clear (the collapse is a response to Jesus' "I am," a theologically loaded formula of self-designation used often in this gospel).

Jesus commands that his disciples not be included in the arrest. His apprehension involves only himself. He rebukes Peter when he strikes out at the servant of the high priest—not because he is opposed to violence, as in Matthew, or because he is concerned about the servant's ear, as in Luke. He rebukes Peter because Peter is frustrating the will of God. The rebuke was doubtless confusing to Peter, who imagined himself to be helping a friend at great personal risk to himself.

The ancient world had no district attorneys, and the accusatory role in Jesus' trial is played by Jewish leadership (the best rendition of John's simple pharase, "the Jews"). The impression is sustained that the Jewish leadership was determined to see Jesus put to death. Its role in the trial passage is largely that of presenting grounds (with some shifting) on which a capital sentence might be secured from Roman authority. The story is the curious but not unfamiliar mixture of searching for legal reasons for doing an immoral act.

Only in this gospel is the Jewish leadership represented as appealing so cravenly to Roman power and authority—"we have no king but Caesar." Such words are more likely to be a literary device indicating the desperation of Jesus' accusers than a representation of even the more quisling elements of Jewish leadership. Creative imagination, serving theological intent, played a substantial role in John's contribution to the passion tradition.

Jesus' worthy antagonist at the trial is Pilate. He is the representative of a great empire, commander of the highest civil power in Palestine. In this account, he makes an articulate foil whose questions and incomprehension provide Jesus with ample opportunity to state as much as he wishes about himself. Pilate occasions no similar pronouncements in the synoptic accounts of the trial.

Vv. 17–41 of chap. 19 show many features which are shared with the synoptic tradition as well as other traces with claim to a pre-Johannine history. Raymond Brown's excellent commentary (*The Gospel According to John, xiii–xxi*, The Anchor Bible, vol. 29A [Garden City, N.Y.: Doubleday & Co., Inc., 1970]) is a rich source for the exploration of this material. A four-gospel synopsis of the passion events makes happy prospecting indeed for a serious student.

The actual details of the death of Jesus have been a source of endless speculation and conjecture in both the first and the twentieth centuries, as well as all those in between. This gospel account is strikingly reticent –"they crucified him" (19:18). A more circumstantial account was not needed; readers could supply the detail. Jesus died by crucifixion. He died among criminals. His executioners gambled for his clothing. Only a few followers (mainly women, including his mother) were present. He was tormented by thirst. He cried one final word: "Finished."

The drama of the passion has many participants. Three persons not yet mentioned may have meaning for us. They are: (1) Judas, who had sealed his own fate by taking action against Jesus (thus fulfilling criminal tendencies shown as early in the record as 12:6); (2) Peter, who enacts the denial of Jesus which was predicted in 13:38; and (3) the "other disciple," who in addition to his appearance in this story is included in 12:23; 19:26; 20:2; 21:7, 20, 24.

This "other disciple" is most interesting. He is depicted as a good friend of Peter. Beside helping him here in this story, he asks Jesus a question for Peter (13:23 f.). Together with Peter he runs to the tomb when he hears that the stone has been removed (20:2). He is the first to recognize Jesus in the post-resurrection scene and tell Peter who it is (21:7). Finally, at the end of the gospel, Peter inquires as to what will be the fate of this disciple (21:20–22). The only appearance made by the "other disciple" without Peter is at the foot of the cross, where he is given responsibility for the mother of Jesus (19:26 f.).

This "other disciple" seems to be an invention of the evangelist. There is no equivalent figure in the synoptics. This device allows the writer to place a character totally of his own making within the Jesus story. The character remains anonymous, functioning chiefly as a kind of alter ego to Peter. He in fact often makes it possible for Peter to come closer to Jesus. He never fails. No aspersions are cast upon his conduct. Quite the opposite; in the language of the evangelist, he is singled out as the disciple whom Jesus loved, the one of whom Jesus said, "If it should be my will that he wait until I come, what is it to you?"

So in this pericope the Good Friday story is not only about Jesus but also about the people around him. One of them can betray him. Another can deny him before a charcoal fire, yet later be restored. Some remain as a community, ready in continuing love when the life here shattered on a cross returns among them. John saw all of this rich human variety—loyalty and disloyalty, insight and impercipience—in the entourage of Jesus.

HOMILETICAL INTERPRETATION

The readings for Good Friday begin with the last, the longest, the most complex, and the greatest of the servant songs. The servant is commonly referred to as the suffering servant. But the depiction of him as a suffering figure is almost entirely dependent on this song. Previously we have seen him as rejected and vindicated (50:5–9), but the servant as sufferer dominates the First Lesson for today.

The song provides an interpretation of that most irrational, apparently purposeless, destructive feature of experience: suffering. Suffering, this song announces, can have a redemptive outcome. It can be utilized by God in the accomplishment of his design. It can widen and deepen moral experience. It can alter the awareness of whole communities. Such an outcome is not automatic. Not all suffering is redemptive. But the things which this song says about meaning in suffering have made a permanent mark on the consciousness of the race.

The song is not abstract. There is no theorizing about suffering or the problem of evil. Rather the song depicts one concrete personal demonstration. One figure is set before us in vivid, circumstantial form. The awareness of suffering is enriched through the discovery of unguessed possibility in what actually happened through the experience of this one—and the community in relation to him.

Indeed, one of the most fascinating and profound features of this song is the interaction of the servant and the community. Most of the song (essentially from 53:1 to the end) is in the voice of the community—what others saw in the servant, what they apprehended concerning themselves through him, what they perceived about God. We usually think of suffering as the most individual of experiences. One encounters it alone. In its depths, no one else can share it. No account can fully represent its pain. It isolates us from one another. Much of this characteristic is present in the servant's suffering. He is alone. He is cut off from a community of understanding, sympathy, and support (53:3, 8 f.). Yet ultimately he is seen as a representative figure. He stands in the most intimate relationship to others: "By his knowledge shall the righteous one, my servant, make many to be accounted righteous" (53:11). What happens to one has effects for the many. The many see the one and recognize themselves in him. He stood for them, and they were in him. He was a paradigmatic person, having a deep mutuality with a community (53:4–6). His solitary, responsible obedience changed the situation of all.

This feature of the song is close to our experience. Surely there are moments when people are so identified in a common life that what happens to one is felt by all. A family, a neighborhood, a city, a nation, can be deeply caught up in the success or the tragedy of one of its members. One person may, through force of character, seize a moral initiative, grasp the imagination of a community, and by his words or actions interpret for the many the meaning of their historical situation—a situation whose meaning would otherwise go unrecognized.

But the great factor that gives redemptive meaning to this suffering is not individual or social; it is the participation of God. Suffering is usually thought of as the factor in existence which thwarts the purpose of God. It is a sign of the absence or the powerlessness of God. But such views are, by biblical reckoning, superficial. In his suffering, this song maintains, the servant is carrying out a vocation to which he is appointed and in which God is identified. He expresses the purpose and character of God (53:10). The way of redemptive suffering is the way of God in bringing to fulfillment his designs within a sinful world. Life, even God's life, as it seeks its deepest expression must engage (and engage sacrificially) with the awesome, life-denying power of evil and suffering.

This servant song came into prominence in the NT as the early church sought a context in which to understand the death of the Messiah and Lord. Not all of the specific details depicting the servant are repeated in the accounts and interpretations of Jesus. But there is a deep, inner correspondence between the two figures. The importance of this servant song is apparent in NT narrative, preaching, and theology. One had come who had suffered cruelly. He had borne it patiently as a role given him in the mysterious purposes of God (53:7; cf. Acts 8:32 f.). A community had come to understand itself as having been involved in what had happened to this one, as he was involved in it (53:5 f.; cf. 1 Pet. 2:24 f.). This one had been vindicated by God and honored in a people. The Christian account of the redemptive meaning of Christ took much of its form from this extraordinary prophetic poem. A Christian's understanding of his own suffering derives its specific character from identification with the suffering Redeemer and from the OT vision by which he is interpreted.

In the Second Lesson for today, the author of Hebrews notes the prevalence of blood in the OT. He cites the crucial incident (Exod. 24:6–8) in which Moses, at the enactment of the first covenant, purified the altar, the lawbook, and the people with blood. But throughout the priestly, sacrificial system (which is the author's principal body of reference), blood is widely used. "Indeed, under the law almost everything is purified by blood." It is an essential element of sin offering. "Without the shedding of blood there is no forgiveness of sins."

The background for this use of blood in the dealings of holy God and sinful man is doubtless the idea that one who breaks the law acquires a kind of ritual contamination or defilement. He is cut off from God as long as the condition persists. By making the right sacrifice, the pollution is removed, and communion with God is restored.

For many modern readers, this element is one of the least appealing features (if it is not actually the most offensive feature) of the OT literature. It all seems so crude and mechanical. What can such ideas have to do with preaching Christ today? How can such themes fit into Holy Week?

Two suggestions might be made here:

1. The image of sin as soiling or defilement contains an important ingredient in the biblical analysis of the human situation. It is not enough to say that the moral problem is this willful act or that—considered in isolation or all added together. We cannot fully correct our moral state, even by doing better from this point on. The act emerges from a condition or character. It is superficial to deal with the acts in themselves. Selfish acts give evidence of a self with problems. The analysis of sin as pollution, while it is subject to its own submoral distortions, speaks to the profound sense that what is wrong with me is me. It goes beyond the facile moralism of salvation by self-improvement. I do not need to mend my foolish ways; I need to be a new person. What I most need, I cannot supply, for I am the source of the dilemma. I need something beyond myself—a gift from another, a sense of being made new.

2. The sacrificial system of the OT, despite its vulnerability, was a gift of God ("This is the blood of the covenant *which God commanded you*," v. 20). It was good news. A way was available for sinners. Self-

reformation and perfection were not divine demands apart from sacrifice as divinely given cleansing.

Seen in this way, the "blood" of the OT way can fittingly speak of Christ. No matter how deep the stain (one thinks of the classic instance of Lady Macbeth's hands), a cleansing is available. Christians used this image of what had taken place in Christ out of a sense that in him they were made clean, made new, restored to God.

When we turn to the Good Friday Gospel passage, we observe that chaps. 18 and 19 of John present a connected narrative. The material is readily divisible into paragraphs and episodes, but the reader is drawn on from Jesus' arrest and trial through his crucifixion and burial. No detail delays us for long. The passion story was doubtless retold in the early church as a unity, and it found its place in the written gospels as an already established account with a beginning, middle, and end. During many centuries of the liturgical tradition, the passion has been read in Holy Week. The narrative still keeps its power to hold and move a Christian hearer.

The passion account in the Fourth Gospel has a number of distinctive features. A partial list might include the following points: The story of Jesus' arrest contains special details. The Jewish trial is virtually eliminated. A dialogue with Pilate is given in detail. Several memorable sayings belong to this account alone: "I am he"; "My kingdom is not of this world"; "What is truth?"; "Behold the man"; and most notably, "I thirst" and "It is finished." Jesus' provision for his mother is not elsewhere recounted. The spear thrust is spoken of only in John. The burial account here brings in Nicodemus.

In addition, the general angle of vision by which the passion is interpreted is not that of the synoptics. There is no Gethsemane agony and prayer and no cry of dereliction. Jesus is always self-possessed and in charge of the events that take place around him. His going to his death is essentially voluntary. Several OT prophecies are unique to John. The background chronology does not put the upper room discourses of chaps. 13–16 in a Passover setting. Rather, Jesus' trial takes place on the eve of Passover; his death coincides with the slaying of the paschal lamb; and his burial is hurried so as not to profane the feast.

The ways of Christian storytelling give little attention to distinguishing sources. As the passion narrative is held in the Christian community's memory, events which are peculiar to the Fourth Gospel have been conflated with material from the synoptic accounts. Many Christians who have heard and read these two narratives, the synoptic and the Johannine, many times are unaware of the special character of either.

It would be safe to guess that much preaching from the passion narratives similarly moves between the first three gospels and the fourth with little awareness of the shift. Yet the material of John 18 and 19 has its own integrity. It presents events from a generally coherent point of view. A preacher, in his own serious examination of the Johannine text, may miss its specific message and power by failing to consider its independent character and point of view. The author is saying something about Jesus that is not just what the other evangelists are saying. He deserves to be heard and preached from out of his own intentions. Cross-references and comparisons usually confuse congregations in this matter. Flat rules would probably eliminate many good sermons. But when preaching from the Fourth Gospel, it would seem desirable to accept the sequence of events, the terms, and the presentation of Jesus of this one rich source and work within them. The Fourth Gospel has a way of interpreting itself. When the Johannine point of view is grasped sympathetically, it is not confining. It is a challenging, compelling encounter with one way of stating the Christian claim for Christ.

What then is the passion story of John saying? What does this account—in its obvious mixture of event and interpretation—urge as the evangelical meaning of Christ's death?

This account develops through its narrative the theme that Christ's death was voluntary. The initiative lay with Jesus. His death was a self-sacrifice. He was in control of his own arrest (18:1–11). He identified himself to the soldiers. Judas was present but did and said nothing. Jesus overwhelmed the arresting group with "I am," indicating that power to free himself was at his disposal. He set the terms for his arrest, enabling his followers to go free. In a similar way, he is in control of his own trial (18:19–24; 18:28–19:11). Others ask questions. Jesus answers in such a way as to turn the interrogation in directions of his choosing and create opportunities for his own self-declarations. This emphasis on Jesus' passion as self-directed is probably suggested in Jesus "bearing his own cross" (19:17). It is certainly sustained in the final clauses: "He said, 'It is finished'; and he bowed his head and gave up his spirit" (19:30). His life was not wrung from him by others. It was his to hold and to yield.

This emphasis is not that of the other gospels, and it raises historical questions. In John, Jesus' initiative is not without realism. It is not stated in such a way as to remove responsibility from the Jewish leaders who "delivered" Jesus to the Roman power or from Pilate who authorized an unjust execution (19:11). These are real actors in a real moral drama. But the Johannine portrait shows Jesus as serene and self-possessed. The Jewish leaders, against Jesus, fell into a rapid degradation that culminated in "We have no king but Caesar." Pilate's weakness and irresponsibility are not minimized. But the moving force is Jesus, by whom all others are tested.

This view of the passion is supported in the Fourth Gospel by the sense that, in these tragic events, God was at work. Jesus may have been the initiator of events at one level, but at a deeper level he was the obedient agent of the long-laid redemptive purpose of the Father. This wider context of interpretation pervades the narrative. The relation of Jesus to God and the identification of his purposes with God's purposes is indicated directly at a number of points: the "I am" of 18:6, the "cup" which the Father has given and Jesus must drink (18:11), Jesus' claim to be a witness to the truth and to be heard by those who are "of the truth" (18:37), Jesus' confident remark that Pilate could have no power over him except it had been given him from above (19:11). Jesus was not a chip afloat in the swirl of history. He was God's man, doing God's work in the midst of the conflict which his own presence had precipitated. He was rooted in and transparent to the will and truth of God.

But indirect hints further support the sense that momentous spiritual events are afoot. The fondness of this evangelist for multiple meanings, which was noted earlier in the week, leads a reader to look for overtones, implications, and suggestions. When Jesus goes over the Kidron valley, he is taking the steps of David, who left the city by this way to return later as a victor (2 Sam. 15:23). When Pilate says, "Here is the man!" (19:5), and asks, "Where are you from?" (19:9), did he not speak more than he knew? This gospel alone notes that Jesus' tunic was seamless (19:23). Should we catch an echo of a fact, reported by Josephus (*Ant.* 11.7, 4) and perhaps widely known, that the high priest's robe was seamless? Caiaphas gives prudential advice that it would be expedient for one man to die for the people (18:14). Was he not inadvertently speaking of the one dying for the sins of the many (see 11:49–51)? The frequent citations of the OT (19:24, 28, 36, 37) locate the passion events in a prefiguring, interpreting context. They are prepared events. The soldiers leaving Jesus' legs unbroken is connected with the treatment of the paschal lamb (19:36, citing Exod. 12:46), implying a redemptive, sacrificial meaning.

A few symbolic meanings in John may contain forward references to the Christian era (out of which the writing came and for which it was intended). Since early Christian times it has been thought that by the three languages of the inscription over the cross (19:20), the author may have intended the universal significance of Jesus and his death. The man from Nazareth would be known to the whole world. Some commentators see in Jesus' giving the care of his mother over to his beloved disciple (19:26 f.) a transfer of the values of Judaism (Jesus' heritage) to the Christian community (Jesus' true brothers and followers). Very likely the blood and water from Jesus' side (19:34) imply the Christian sacraments, with a deeply realistic sense of their significance. The redemption won in Christ's death is present and available in the community shaped by a "water" ritual of entry (baptism) and sustained by a "blood" ritual of life (the Holy Communion).

Some of these overtones and suggestions are more debatable than others. More possibilities than have been hinted here might be suggested. How convincing this line of interpretation of the Fourth Gospel is depends largely on how well one thinks it captures a style of thinking which pervades the book.

If this large context is implicit in John's passion narrative, it is saying some massively important things. In this one life whose witness to truth brought opposition, conflict, and death at the hands of enemies, God was acting. This man who was mocked, whose last possessions were taken by his executioners, who agonized in thirst, Jesus of Nazareth, was heir of God's ancient purpose—the world's high priest and true king. He was the one from God, acting in God's power. His death was life for many—a true paschal offering. When he said, "It is finished," he declared the culmination of the redemptive purpose of eternal God.